THE

INTEI IMPACT
CONUNDRUM

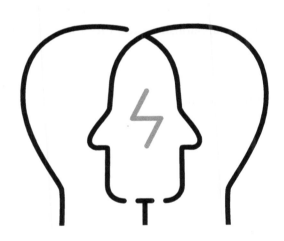

PRACTICAL WAYS TO ACHIEVE
THE IMPACT YOU WANT

FLORENCE MADDEN

Printed in the United Kingdom

First Printing, 2018

ISBN 978-1-9996460-0-4 (Print)
ISBN 978-1-9996460-1-1 (eBook)

Florence Madden Associates
Orchard Syke
Unthank, Dalston
Carlisle, Cumbria
CA5 7BA

www.florencemadden.co.uk

PRAISE FOR "THE INTENTION IMPACT CONUNDRUM"

"A great 'bringing together' of ways of thinking that result in simple, practical ways of learning and living in harmony with the world. What more could you ask?"
— **Sue Knight,** NLP Master Trainer and author of 'NLP at Work'

"As a trainer and coach Florence inspires and empowers you to be your best. I wondered if the 'magic' she delivers in person could be brought to life in a book - yes it can! The humour and insight that Florence brings to the practice of NLP makes things 'click' and leaves a lasting impact. The book introduces you to the very exciting prospect of being able to change from within."
— **Dr Jo Verrill,** Managing Director, Ceeda.

"Powerful, practical and de-mystifying how to be personally effective! A brilliant guide how to manage others and motivate them to be their best version of themselves! Apply Florence's suggestions and you'll feel much more empowered and equipped in your day to day tasks. Her straight-forward approach and accessible format of the book make this a must-have in the office."
— **Eleni Sarantinou**, author of 'Perception Projection, 9 principles to empower your team' and co-author of 'Everyday NLP'

"A brilliant compilation of models and theories supported by practical explanations and real life examples of what they mean for the reader. Each time I revisit a chapter I think of another thing that I can do to get the most from my interactions with others!"
— **Maureen Tallis,** Head of Employee Development for Baxi Heating UK Limited

"I love this book… a delicate blend of theory and practical application that guides the reader through reviewing the impact of theirs and others behaviours. I particularly enjoyed being prompted to take stock and reflect as I read. A great read as an introduction to NLP or as a refresher. Well Done - you've written a fabulous book!?
— **Laura Cadman,** Chief Executive Officer, Cumbria CVS

"A book to change your thinking (and maybe your life)! Florence generously and skilfully shares her knowledge and experience of human interaction through stories and real examples, giving you all the tools you need to maximise your everyday impact."
— **Claire Bradshaw,** Executive Coach and Development Consultant

"Taking time out to read this book will transform the way you approach work and life too. A totally refreshing and engaging read that will enhance and improve your outlook and ways of thinking & doing!"
— **Chris Bray,** Head of Marketing and Income Generation, Eden Valley Hospice and Jigsaw Cumbria's Children's Hospice

"I really gobbled up this book…it's so practical and I know I would want to go back and read it over to prepare or keep positive when feeling wobbly. The chapter on language was really helpful and the examples are great. The book is like having Florence in my back pocket! This book will reach so many more folk and I know will make massive difference for those looking to make change."
— **Nicky Ellis,** Well-being, Behaviour and Safeguarding Lead

"An accessible and insightful guide to the important work of mastering our effect on other people."
— **Dr David Fraser,** Leadership team coach and author of 'The Mastery of Leadership'

"My hope is that this book finds its way onto the training programmes of managers and H.R. Teams everywhere and in every sphere of working life… make it YOUR 'intention' to focus on the 'impact' and unravel the conundrums which exist in all relationships."
— **Alyson Renwick,** Nurture Teacher, Glasgow North East

Contents

"The World is full of magic things patiently waiting for our senses to grow sharper"

WB Yeats

WB Yeats lived for a period of his life close to his friends the Gore-Booth sisters in Lissadell Co Sligo. They were near neighbours and contemporaries of my mother's in her early years. His poetry still makes an impact on me.

Chapter 1
What's The Problem?

THE VIEW FROM HERE

When you stand inside a building usually you can see what is in there, you know the quality of the light, the temperature, the furnishings – and something of what it is like to be in there. People outside can only glimpse through the windows or other openings and see only a little of what you can see. They can only guess what it is like to be in there, based on what they observe. From inside we don't have their perspective either, we don't know the overall picture that they can see or interpret how it looks to them.

That is how it is for us too as people. We know what it is like on the inside because that is our main view. Sometimes we don't even know what is in some of the rooms yet, because we have to make the effort to explore those rooms to know what is there. We don't know what people are seeing from the outside unless we go out and join them there, and ask them questions about what they are seeing. So our view, if we stand still, is naturally limited. In NLP[1] a key pre-supposition is that:

Everyone has a different map of the world

If on the other hand we are curious enough to explore, paying attention to what is happening around us, willing to shift our perspective and are respectful enough to ask for and listen to others' viewpoints, then our map of the world will expand and change! With it, our relationships with others, and indeed with ourselves, shifts too.

That is what this book is all about

… being curious
… being willing to look from new perspectives
… being open to feedback verbal or observed
… and helping others to do the same…

So how can we get a handle on the impact we have on others… and what to do about it? A model that provides a useful way to capture the 'intention impact conundrum' is Johari Window. This is a model created in the 1950s by psychologists **Jo**seph Luft and **Harri**ngton Ingham, (who clearly had some marketing advice in naming their creation!)

It is worth acknowledging that the Johari Window is a simplified way of looking at human behaviour, nonetheless, I think it is a useful starting point for looking at how we might be seen by others.

Their idea was that how we impact on others is an interplay of two factors:

- Firstly, how much self-knowledge we have i.e. **how open to feedback**
- Secondly how much of ourselves and our opinions that **we choose to share** with others.

This creates 4 window 'panes':

- The Public Arena
- The Hidden/Private Area
- The Blind Area
- The Unknown/Potential area

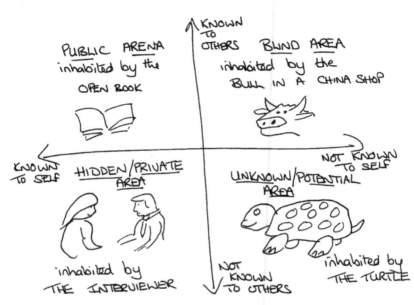

When we have good self-knowledge, we achieve this by both being open to feedback and taking feedback on board rather than ignoring or denying it. In that way, we start to build a clearer picture of how we are seen by others and how we impact on them. When we know this we have a choice as to what we do about it, but the key point is that it is an informed choice. On the other hand, if we deny or avoid feedback, we are in the dark and so our choices are limited.

When we are open with others we are willing to share our thoughts, ideas and opinions with others, as well as information about ourselves. This would also include giving feedback to others too. When we do this, we also find that we get feedback. For example, when we offer our thoughts and ideas respectfully and openly in a meeting, it is likely to create discussion and encourage openness in others too. Maybe some people agree with us or maybe not, either way, we are likely to draw out more of their thinking. When we share our ideas we get feedback that may indicate that they are unworkable, or conversely find that they catch others' imaginations and maybe they can build on these. If we don't share them though we might never know!

There is a story I often relate on courses about a communications company in North America that had cables running across the tundra in Canada. When the winter snow came the weight of snow often broke the cables, creating an expensive repair job. It was a problem that a group were working on in a meeting when someone suggested: "Why don't we get the polar bears to shake the poles!" His idea wasn't fully fledged... and maybe his colleagues did chuckle at the idea – but crucially they started to build on it by asking questions. Firstly, how do we get the polar bears to do that? He suggested putting some food on the top of the pole, to which the answer came 'what kind of food...and won't it spoil?' He thought again and came up with the idea of putting honey on top of the poles. That would work they agreed ...but how do you get it up there on so many poles? At this point, a colleague came into the room that had been in Vietnam during the war and she suggested dropping the honey from a helicopter (which was how they accessed difficult places during the war). Another colleague pointed out that the down draught from the helicopter would blow the honey off its intended target... and at that point, they realised it would blow the snow off the wires too!!

So thanks to one person being willing to test his idea...and his colleagues being willing to pursue it ... they had their answer. Often we may not see what impact we can have with our ideas and our intention of protecting ourselves from the criticism or ridicule that we fear, can hold us back from making that impact.

So our window 'panes' are flexible depending on how much we open ourselves to feedback in all its forms, and how willing we are to share information. Luft and Ingham propose that we can present ourselves in four different ways making quite different impacts on those around us... as well as on ourselves of course. Each of these is a description of what happens depending on the choices we make, they represent what happens in the extreme, although we may exhibit these traits in a milder form.

The Ideal – 'The Open Book'

People we describe in this way are prepared to be open to feedback verbal or otherwise, even asking others directly for it and are willing to consider what they hear or observe. This has two key effects:

- First of all, they have more information about themselves and therefore more choice as to what they do about it.
- Secondly, being open to others' feedback, and especially when they have asked for it, can significantly enhance the relationship with those people. It is a great expression of trust and even esteem to ask others for their view.

It is pretty important of course that those we ask know in advance that we are prepared to take the feedback on board – we need to make it 'safe' for others to tell us what they really think. People don't like to give complimentary feedback that is dismissed or critical feedback that is 'talked away' i.e. when the receiver offers excuses or denials. (See Chapter 5).

Similarly, people who spend most of their time in this Ideal/Open Book 'pane' are prepared to share their thoughts, ideas and (appropriate!) personal information with others – and pay attention to the response they get. No guess work here – other people know what they are thinking and this can promote more trust and openness in the relationship.

Luft and Ingham unsurprisingly called this their 'ideal' window pane, and in my experience, people who behave consistently in this way have better relationships with others. The 'gap' between their **intention** and their **impact** is at its narrowest, so they know and are more in control of what is happening between themselves and others.

In theory, this makes sense, in practice it is not always easy to do. So we can fall into presenting ourselves through the other windows and this has consequences for how we impact on others… and ultimately on ourselves.

'The Interviewer'

People we describe in this way are open to feedback about themselves and hearing other people's views. In fact, they ask a lot of questions – hence the name 'The Interviewer'!

Initially, this person's apparent interest in us can feel good. Over a period of time, however, the fact that this is not reciprocated, with this person sharing their views and ideas, this feeling can shift dramatically. Most delegates on courses tell me that this would lead them to be mistrustful of this person and particularly in a work environment, they would be quite suspicious of their motives. Their reaction to this is to put a bit of distance between themselves and the 'Interviewer'.

When I challenge this and ask 'how do you know the person is going to do anything detrimental with this information?' the reply is that they don't – nonetheless, they would still feel this way! In Chapter 5, I refer to the 'negativity' bias that is evident in humans and this is likely to be at work here.

I received a really useful piece of feedback when I was discussing this in a course one day: a delegate said to me "Florence, you are a bit of an interviewer!" He had a bit of mischief in his eye as he said it and yet my internal dialogue went along the lines of 'I am a coach… this is my job… I am supposed to ask you questions to get you to think etc.' Fortunately I didn't say any of this as at the same time I recognised it doesn't matter that I am facilitating this course and he is a delegate, we are adult human beings having a conversation.

Whether his point was for comic effect or not... it was still a valid one and one that I have reflected on and been grateful for many times since. Crucially it has shifted my awareness and my style, (I hope for the better). It definitely brought the gap between my intention and my impact into sharp focus!

'The Bull In A China Shop'

'The Bull' is perhaps the opposite to the Interviewer. (Reminds me of the Shakespeare observation 'those in the extremity of either are abominable fellows'!)

People whose behaviour is predominantly in this 'windowpane', will most certainly share their views, opinions and personal information liberally. In doing so they are likely to be missing the signals from others, i.e. if they do not want this information, or they have information of their own to share. Perhaps worse still some 'Bulls' may ask for feedback and then tell the giver why they are wrong. That approach closes down direct verbal feedback to the 'Bull' pretty rapidly and can even redirect it into the unhelpful realm of gossip with others, particularly if the feedback giver is frustrated or feels unheard.

This could happen with feedback that is complimentary, which is dismissed as flattery, or critical which can be explained away or denied. The result of this is not just that the 'Bull's' self-knowledge remains limited, but it can also damage the credibility or acceptability of the feedback they give to others. That's a pity as those people in turn, then also lose out on valuable information too.

'The Turtle'

Turtles have a shell which covers most of their body. We think about the shell as being for protection when in fact palaeontologists believe that its original purpose was to support its ability to dig. Whatever its purpose the very thing that protects it also hides it from the outside world and so it is for human turtles!

People who behave 'like Turtles' keep themselves to themselves, minimising the information they share with others. In work situations they are likely to keep their views and ideas to themselves, perhaps leading others to underestimate them and often to ignore them. It feels like hard work to draw their contribution. Perhaps because of this, others are likely to be reluctant to give feedback and they are unlikely to ask for it.

So their true potential stays untapped – not known to others and probably not known to themselves either. The very thing that protects, also severely limits. One course delegate told me "I am really an Open Book inside but behave like a Turtle on the outside!" I think a lot of us can understand that, as frequently it is the environment and perceptions of it that can put, or keep, someone in their shell.

PUTTING OURSELVES AT 'CAUSE'

So how can we know where we are at any point and how we are impacting on others?

In explaining each of these 'window panes' I have exaggerated to make a point and the likelihood is that we don't just stay in one, instead we inhabit different windows in different circumstances. And that is the point, only in the first pane 'the Open Book' are our relationships at their most effective. Circumstances and our reaction to them can allow us (perhaps unknowingly) to drop into one of the others with the corresponding deterioration of our impact! We can allow ourselves to become a 'hostage to fortune' with our impact being determined by other people or circumstances, and not necessarily our conscious choice.

A key concept in NLP is the idea of Cause > Effect. When we put ourselves at *Effect* we can end up blaming everything else but ourselves for the situations we find ourselves in and therefore those people/circumstances have to change in order for things to change for us. That is a process we have no control over. Similarly, we can end up blaming ourselves. Really, both of these positions signal a lack of choice on our part, and perhaps more accurately an unawareness of the choices we have.

On the other hand when we put ourselves at *'Cause'*[2] i.e. in the sense of asking ourselves 'what is my part in this and what can I do about it?', then we move ourselves into a much more resourceful position. Here we can develop alternatives and test them out – the basis of personal responsibility.

(Incidentally, you may also have observed that when an individual is at cause they are easier to be around too.)

Nonetheless being open to feedback, asked for or otherwise, feels like such a risk, but does not knowing it exposes us to risk by default? Verbal feedback is not our only source, of course, when we pay attention to our own response in situations and notice that of others, we become more aware of what is working and what needs to change. I often quote (the great philosopher) Elizabeth Taylor with her famous line from the Tennessee Williams play 'Cat On Hot Tin Roof':

"Not looking at a fire doesn't put it out!" …So it is with feedback surely?

It can also feel like a risk to share information about yourself or offer your ideas – if you don't though, that may restrict your feedback or your ideas, and perhaps by default, adversely affect your development. To quote Martha Graham the dancer and choreographer:

"There is vitality, a life force, an energy, a
quickening, that is translated through you
into action, and because there is only one of
you in all time, this expression is unique."

Martha was talking about dance of course, which is simply another form of self-expression. Unless we put our thoughts and ideas out there, the world will not have them. My friend and associate Eleni Sarantinou said pretty much the same thing to me when we discussed my writing this book. So as I write this I am wondering how this book will impact on you, your thinking and your actions! Knowing where we are (and which 'windows' we are occupying) is a sound start to any journey...isn't it?

As each Chapter unfolds I will discuss ways in which you can choose to be more in the ideal 'Open Book' pane and therefore get more of the impact on others that you want.

ENDNOTES

1. NLP – Neuro Linguistic Programming is an approach to communication, personal development, and psychotherapy created by Richard Bandler, John Grinder and Frank Pucelik in California, the United States in the 1970s.

    Their work was based on the work of thinkers in 1960s and 1970s operating in the fields of cybernetics[3], therapy and philosophy. NLP Presuppositions help to frame how we see ourselves, other people and situations in a more resourceful way.

    There are numerous references to NLP and NLP Pre-suppositions and approaches throughout this book.

2. 'At Cause': for clarity, I use this term throughout the book to mean taking personal responsibility rather than taking the blame in situations. This is an important distinction and a key choice to make.

3. Cybernetics – the branch of science concerned with control systems in electronic and mechanical devices and the extent to which useful comparisons can be made between man-made and biological systems. (Ref Collins Dictionary)

Exercise:

1. Take some time to think about how you present yourself to the outside world and even ask some friends or colleagues how they see you.

2. You may notice that one 'pane' may dominate – who or what moves you out of that and to what effect? In these circumstances are you 'at Cause' or 'at Effect'?

KEY POINTS:

» We have a unique view of and from ourselves which is distinctly different from what other people see… and we don't see what they see either

» How we are seen is to a large degree down to us: how much we choose to reveal to others and how open we are to feedback

» Being the 'Open Book' is most likely to make our relationships stronger and more effective

» Being the 'Interviewer' may create mistrust of us in others

» Being the 'Bull In a China Shop' is likely to frustrate others and cause them to avoid us, as we may not take their feedback on board and therefore not modify our behaviour

» Being the 'Turtle', keeping our views and ideas under our 'shell' may lead others to underestimate us and hamper our development

» Recognising what we are doing, being willing to take responsibility and putting ourselves 'At Cause', as opposed to 'At Effect', is a great start in making our impact match our intention!

Chapter 2
This Is How It Is...
Isn't It?

SO WHAT IS REALITY?

In the first chapter, I started with the metaphor of us being inside a house and seeing it from that perspective, whilst others are looking in from the outside. My point, of course, was that to manage our impact, we need to recognise that regardless of any good intentions on our part what others experience of us, is *how it is for them* – and they behave accordingly.

In this chapter, I want to take this a stage further by looking more closely at how we make up the picture of our own reality.

Let's just look at this idea of 'reality' for the moment. A delegate on a course once said to me mischievously: "But of course in the real world, Florence…" I replied (also with a twinkle in my eye), "What makes you think that the world I inhabit is not real?" He laughed and admitted he hadn't thought about it that way.

We all see the world through the prism of our experiences… and they are unique to us. Even though we may have siblings brought up in the same household, we may have different educational experiences. When we leave home we are likely to live in different places, go to different places on holiday, have our own relationships and have a whole myriad of different life experiences. After all that whilst there will be some things that we agree on, it would be miraculous if we all saw everything in the same way. And those are people with the same roots as us – how much more differently will others from different families, different areas and different parts of the world see things from the way we do?

As Fran Burgess notes in her book "The Bumper Book of Modelling" one of the underpinning theories of NLP is a branch of philosophy called Constructivism. A central assumption of Constructivism is that people uniquely create their own realities or models of the world based on their life experiences. We internally order our experiences into organised patterns or structures. Simply put, we each experience the world in our own unique way and it can be a big mistake in our relationships to assume others see things in the same way as we do. In NLP we summarise this with the presuppositions:

- Everyone has a different map of the world
- The map is not the territory[1]

In other words how we see things is not necessarily how it is... simply our internal representation of a person or a situation for example.

A very common way in which we see this is when we listen to people debate a topic. Whichever point of view we may favour at the outset, when another puts forward their view in a compelling (and respectful) way, we may not necessarily change our view, but we may understand more clearly why they hold theirs. Usually, an episode of BBC's Question Time can illustrate this point well!

So how do our experiences influence us and how we see the world around us? To answer that question we need to look at how the brain processes the information it receives.

HOW THE BRAIN FILTERS OUR WORLD

To look at how the brain filters our experiences let's look at Tad James and Wyatt Woodsmall's model overleaf. This was developed from the work of Richard Bandler and John Grinder and sets out how information coming into our brain is filtered, creating our own unique view of things and ultimately how we present ourselves to the outside world:

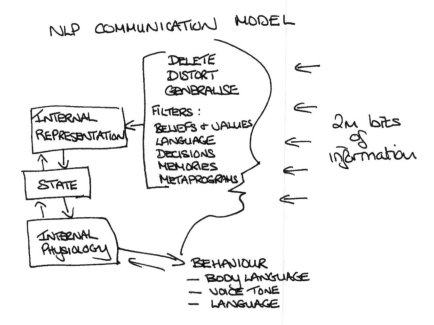

We have over 2 million bits of information a second coming into our brain, more than our conscious mind can process. So the brain acts as a sort of reducing valve and by the time something comes into our conscious mind, the unconscious has refined it and given it a meaning. Noam Chomsky (sometimes referred to as 'the father of modern linguistics') explained that the brain filters the information by a 3 part process of deletion, distortion and generalisation.

Deletion

The unconscious selects what is brought into our conscious awareness and what is left in the background.

We become aware of this process when people draw things to our attention that we hadn't noticed before. You may have experienced when you become interested in a type of car: you start to see more and more on the roads or in car parks; or a holiday destination you hadn't considered before, keeps cropping up in magazines, television programmes or conversations. Those things were always there but your unconscious mind did not consider them worthy of your interest, so they were deleted.

Distortion

Our brain also fits new experiences with what it knows already i.e. patterns of thinking already established. When we look at a cloud, for example, we can start to see shapes – our brain is fitting this abstract shape with ones it knows already. This is really useful in learning because it helps us use our current knowledge to understand new information coming in: if someone is already proficient with a number of software packages, that knowledge will help them when faced with one that is new to them.

Where distortion can cause us problems is when we 'bend' what we hear to fit with an already existing internal pattern. An example of this is when someone gives me directions in an area I know a little, I can find myself fitting what they are saying with my mental map. I am bending what they are saying to fit my pre-held pattern. (It's not just humans of course that I treat in this way; I have on occasion done the same thing with the sat nav in my car!) Unsurprisingly, this often results in getting lost!

Generalisation

The third filter is generalisation: taking an instance and making a general rule from it. This is also really useful in our everyday lives if we do not have to relearn basics every day. When we get in the car in the morning (if we are in the UK) we just assume that we, and everyone else, will drive on the left hand side of the road. We may read a number of books from the same author as we assume that if we liked their style previously, that any new book they publish will also be to our taste.

Once again what is valuable in many respects, can also give us a problem, as it means that we can reapply a pattern of thinking in other areas in our lives, often without questioning it. An example of this is if I mention appraisals on courses: I often get a range of facial expressions followed by derisory comments. These opinions of appraisals are based on the individuals' previous bad experience, and as a result, their view of the whole process of appraisal is coloured by that. Similarly, this can work the other way round where previous good experience can lead to an assumption that this is how all appraisals are.

The result of this 3 part filtering process is to narrow and 'customise' our band of what we regard as reality to such an extent that in our conscious awareness most people can only handle 7 pieces of information, plus or minus two at any one time. Just try going to a shop for say ten items without a written list and notice what happens!

So our 'internal representation' of the world around us is what is projected onto the 'movie screen' of our mind, once it has passed through this filter system. Consider shining a white spotlight onto a screen and then passing a filter in front of the light. What light gets through, and what gets projected onto the screen, is determined by the filters. And part and parcel of this filtration process is that we apply our own value and significance to what we perceive and hence our interpretation of events. Moreover, as this process is happening unconsciously, we may not even be aware that how we perceive things is just that… and not necessarily correct. Frequently I hear people say that they 'tell it like it is', apparently unaware that it would be more accurate to add the words 'to me' to the end of their sentence.

In fact so heavily 'interpreted' is our view of the world that it is believed when we recount a conversation or an incident as little as 2-7% of what we say may be factually correct. As a trainer I was dismayed by this figure at first – now when anyone gets anything of what I have said, I get such a thrill. It stops me thinking that just because I think I have set out something clearly, that it is what people have understood. My impact as a trainer, therefore, depends on staying aware and not assuming.

There have been numerous experiments to show the effect of our filters. One experiment was the result of a New York policeman being convicted of collusion with his colleagues. They had been found guilty of beating up a suspect and their colleague who was chasing a felon past the scene, denied that he had seen anything. The court did not believe him. So an experiment was set up in a park to recreate the scene. This time the 'chaser' was an unsuspecting member of the public who was just told to chase the person running in front of him or her. At one point to the side of the path, a mock beating was staged. More than 60% of the chasers failed to notice!

THE CONSCIOUS VERSUS THE UNCONSCIOUS – WHO IS IN CHARGE?

"Albert Einstein called the intuitive or metaphoric mind a sacred gift. He added that the rational mind was a faithful servant. It is paradoxical that in the context of modern life we have begun to worship the servant and defile the divine."

Bob Samples, Scholar, Artist and Author

In spite of our self-awareness… and many of us spend a lot of time working on it… it is estimated that 90% of our behaviour is driven not by our conscious, but our unconscious mind. (See Chapter 7). This was something understood by ancient civilisations but only began to be really understood in modern times in the 20th century. The unconscious has been likened to a 5 year old child seeing things in a simplistic way, needing direction and eager to please. So it is the conscious mind that knows how we want to come across, it sets the direction (like the captain of a ship), it is the unconscious (the crew), that has the power to get us there. And how that unconscious part of our brain filters information coming in determines how we react and what we show to the outside world.

HOW DOES OUR 'STATE' AFFECT OUR IMPACT?

When you look again at the NLP Communication model, you see that the filtering process creates our own internal representation of the information coming into us. Given that part of how information is filtered are the beliefs and values we hold, this affects what interpretation we put on that information.

This interpretation, in turn, affects our emotional state. So if the way in which someone speaks to us seems disrespectful because of what they said, or how they said it, the state could be one of anger. For example, someone could speak to us using language or turn of phrase that reminds us of a previous colleague with whom we had a bad relationship. Our interpretation, therefore, is coloured by that association in our mind.

And the chain reaction continues, as our state affects our internal physiology. The body takes anger as an emergency signal and muscles tense, breathing rate increases and heart rate increases. This reaction is triggered unconsciously and we are into a physiological response to anger before our conscious mind can rationalise about the situation.

Of course what is happening on the inside shows on the outside and our emotional state, therefore, is impacting on others around us even before we say anything. Someone once said to me "Florence when I am angry with someone there is no way they can tell". Well he may be right in as much as some people will display their emotions more readily than others, but the greater likelihood is that there will be some indication, and as animals ourselves, we are likely to pick up the signals at some level. In addition, when we start to speak, our choice of words and voice tone are also going to give more information about our emotional state.

Then, of course, the whole process starts to happen for those who are on the 'receiving end' of us… they start to interpret our behaviour as it impacts on them, and our intention may be quite lost as the reaction of one draws in the other. A friend of mine frequently starts her courses by asking the question "What is it like to be on the receiving end of you?" Many of her audience are starting to think of the answer to that (possibly chilling) question for the first time… it's a thought, isn't it?

DOES IT HAVE TO BE THIS WAY?

In short… no! Key areas where we can intervene and make a change in this process are by:

- Updating our filters by revising our values and beliefs – in effect 'reframing' our views of self and others to take a more resourceful attitude
- Changing the messages to our unconscious by becoming aware of and changing our language
- Becoming aware of and taking control of how we are presenting ourselves physically to others i.e. our body language

As well as what we may do intentionally, of course, our brain also continues (unconsciously) to re-filter the experiences in our lives over time. The result of this is that we naturally review, re-assess and re-interpret events. So often our view of a situation or a person can shift and change as time moves on. This is sometimes described variously as taking a longer view, maturing, or even mellowing. However we name it, clearly, our 'filters' are not fixed but being modified as we progress through life, experiencing new things, learning new things and meeting new people. So as our filters change, information passing through, or being re-filtered, is being interpreted differently.

So read on. As you progress through the rest of this book we will look at ways in which we can take more control of this process, by deliberately making changes in ourselves to manage our impact on others and bring it closer to what we want to achieve.

Robert Dilts says what brought him into the world of NLP was observing:

"...the difference that makes the differ-
ence. When people changed, they moved from
their 'map' to multiple perspectives"

ENDNOTES

1. Originally coined by Polish American Scientist and Philosopher, Alfred Korzybski

Exercise:

You can start now 'updating your filters' by doing this little exercise:

- Look at an object in the room you are in (or wherever you are reading this book). Notice what you can see of it from where you are.
- How would people in another part of the room (or location) see the object that might be different to your view?
- Who would have the 'correct' view? Is there one?
- If you wanted to know more about that object what would you have to do...where would you have to move to?

It seems obvious when we are talking about an object that we would indeed need to move our position – and that anyone claiming the 'correct' view might have an argument on their hands.

What if you apply that same thinking to a subject on which you have differing views to another person? What would happen if you become more curious about seeing it from their angle? What might happen between you and them if you did?

KEY POINTS:

» An underpinning theory of NLP is Constructivism which says that we all create our own 'reality'

» This is captured by two NLP pre-suppositions:
  • Everyone has a different map of the world
  • The map is not the territory

» The NLP Communication Model shows how we filter the 2m bits of information a second by a process of deletion, distortion and generalisation

» As a result, our recollection of a situation or conversation has been heavily interpreted by our brain

» This process is happening unconsciously and the unconscious mind is believed to be driving 90% of our behaviour

» How we interpret conversations affects our 'state' which in turn can provoke a 'state' in others

» We can update our filters through taking on more resourceful beliefs and attitudes, paying attention to the language we use and becoming aware of our body language and its impact on ourselves and others

Chapter 3
Aaaargh... Why Are They Talking To Me Like This?

IS HELL REALLY OTHER PEOPLE?

Jean-Paul Sartre the French novelist and playwright, said "Hell is other people" …or at least a character in his play 'No Exit' thought so. There may be times when we are inclined to agree with him, but it is probably an unhelpful, not to say unfair, mindset.

In the last chapter, I looked at this idea of reality and how we construct our own reality. It isn't surprising then when we are sometimes baffled by the reactions of others or what they say to us. In some more extreme situations, we might even wonder if someone is in their right mind when they speak to us. It may come as a surprise then that everyone, it would seem, thinks they are sane and that their reactions are logical at least in the moment – hindsight might give a different view of course!

An example of this might be the reaction to our parents. As children or teenagers, we might have raged against their views or the things they said to us. Then I often hear people say that they, as parents themselves, find they are saying the same things to their children as their parents said to them. It is not surprising really, as it seems to be the case that our brains are storing up all of the things that we hear, see and feel through our lives. As a result, all of our life experiences go into the making up of our personalities.

So in this Chapter, I want to explore how we start to understand our interactions with others better, and importantly, what we can do to create more effective outcomes for ourselves and others. To do this I am going to refer to the work of psychiatrist Dr Eric Berne and his theory of Transactional Analysis developed in the 1950s, remarkably, a way of understanding human interactions that has stood the test of time. What follows is a quick guide to understanding the principles of Transactional Analysis, to help us to make sense of and create more choice in our interactions with others. There is a great deal more to it and there are a number of reference texts at the end of this book where you can find out more.

SO WHAT CAN TRANSACTIONAL ANALYSIS TELL US ABOUT THE ORIGINS OF PERSONALITY?

Eric Berne was inspired by the work of Dr Wilder Penfield a pioneering neurosurgeon who came up with the idea that the brain is like a recording device, recording every life event and feeling. As any time taking examinations will tell you, we do not remember everything that we have experienced; but remembered or not, it goes to making up our personality. The result is our multi-facetted personality which is influenced by:

- the 'big people' (i.e. parents, teachers, adult relatives and neighbours) in our lives as children
- our own reactions to the world as children
- the thinking we have done for ourselves as we make sense of the world around us.

Berne referred to these as Parent, Adult and Child *Ego states*. (Ego states refer to set of related behaviours, thoughts and feelings that make up our personality at any moment in time.)

I believe the longevity of Berne's ideas has a lot to do with the fact that we already have a shared understanding of what **Parent** behaviour is like. We recognise that those in the parent role sometimes seem very bossy and critical, and at other times caring and self-sacrificing.

Similarly, we know what people mean when they refer to behaviour as *Childish* or *Childlike* – the former being quite irritating and the latter rather sweet, innocent or naive.

When we think of how *Adults* behave, there can be confusion, as we know people who are unrelated to us but can take a Parental role with us and often not to our liking. We also know grownups who behave in childish or childlike ways. Adult behaviour, therefore, is not as stereotyped as Parent or Child. When we think of what Adults behaving as adults might be, then the picture is clearer. We may be thinking that this conjures up pictures of adults expressing their views with confidence and being prepared to listen to others and treat their views with respect, even when they disagree.

So typically in a day, or even in a conversation, we go in and out of these 'Ego' states and probably most people are unaware of the process in the moment. It is hardwired, (i.e. intrinsic and difficult to change), from childhood to react to other people and situations in a particular way. The more we can understand the process and become aware of it, the more able we are to make choices about how we react. So let's look at each ego state in a bit more detail.

RECOGNISING THE PARENT EGO STATE

Think for a moment about the words that pop into your head when you hear the word Parent. Then think about what pictures the word creates – what words or phrases come to mind…

The likelihood is that you think about your own parents, guardians, teachers or yourself as a parent. You may be thinking of the care and also the discipline they brought to your life – and the frustration that you may have felt with both of those things. You may remember the hugs and the finger-wagging – the words of encouragement and laying the law down! The comfort and the annoyance of being around someone who 'knows best'!

If these are the things that you were bringing to mind, Eric Berne would have agreed with you. He identified two sides to the Parent ego state:

- *The Controlling Parent* (sometimes called Critical Parent): when in this ego state people can be stern, forceful or even aggressive with body language and speech patterns to match.
- *The Nurturing Parent*: when in this ego state people can be caring, sympathetic and even self-sacrificing. At times 'thinking for' others rather than letting them work out things for themselves. Their body language and speech also reflect this softer approach.

These parental behaviours make a lot of sense when someone is responsible for the care and guidance of a child. In grown-up relationships, personal or in work environments they take on a different meaning. We learn these behaviours, of course, from the 'big people' around us when we were children.

RECOGNISING THE CHILD EGO STATE

Now think what comes to mind when you hear the word Child. Then think about what pictures this word creates – what words or phrases come to mind...

Your answer to this might be influenced by how much contact you have with children, and the states they are in when you do. You may be thinking about the sweet, innocent imaginative child who fully expects you to know when they ask how helicopters work, or if you can have a tiger as a family pet, or who laughs uncontrollably at something that seems silly to them. A recent visit to a supermarket, on the other hand, may have given you a different view. For example, a child who has been refused something and having a tantrum on the floor, or one who has been sharply reprimanded, hanging their head and close to tears.

Once again if these are similar to your thoughts, you will have spotted, as Berne did, that there are different aspects of the Child ego state:

- *The Free Child* (sometimes called the Natural child): this is believed to be our 'original' state at birth. We are the unwritten page whose only fears are of loud noises and being dropped. In this state, we have no sense of being good or bad, right or wrong. When old enough, we draw things as they are in our heads and we have no sense of 'appropriate' behaviour. In later life remnants of this behaviour will still be there, coming out as creative, innovative or jokey behaviour.

- **_The Adapted Child_**: this develops when parents/guardians start to 'adapt' a child's behaviour by perhaps putting rules or restrictions in place. The result is twofold:
  - _The Rebellious Child_: when in this ego state we see tantrums, sulking and argumentative behaviour in 'children' of all ages, whether four or forty!
  - _The Conforming Child_: when in this ego state we see unsure, submissive or even fearful behaviour, once again behaviour that carries on into later life.

In all of these _Child_ ego states, the body language and speech patterns will match the behaviour. As with the Parent ego state, when these behaviours are seen in actual children they are understandable and even expected. It is logical when you are a child that you want to influence what happens to you, (and when you do not have the option of moving out), you use whatever strategies you have. This behaviour can be seen as manipulative and can have more serious consequences in relationships when the 'child' is grown up.

When others see these behaviours in us as grownups, they are getting a snapshot of us as children.

RECOGNISING THE ADULT EGO STATE

Earlier in this chapter, I referred to the fact that Adult behaviour is the least stereotypical. It can seem like the last part to fully form, although in truth it is developing through our lives as we make sense of the world. It describes our ability to think and rationalise for ourselves and reach our own conclusions about things based on the 'here and now'. Indeed it has the effect, often, of keeping our Parent and Child ego states in check.

We experience emotion when we are in this state, the difference being that we are not at the mercy of it and so don't 'act it out'. This is a state where we respect our own opinions and express them when we choose to, and show respect for the opinions of others. This is reflected in our voice tone and our body language: upright, relaxed and comfortable in our own skin. Unsurprisingly, it is when we are showing this behaviour that others in our relationships and work environments find us easiest to relate to.

A rather nice illustration of the adult ego state in action is an interview conducted by Terry Wogan years ago on his chat show. His guests were the late great footballer, (and sometime party animal), George Best and Sister Wendy Beckett (Nun and Art Historian). At one point Terry asked Sister Wendy to advise George as to what he should do, in the light of some recent scandalous behaviour. She replied that she never uses the words 'ought' and 'should' to anyone other than herself. The producers of the programme had probably expected a parental rush of advice-giving; instead, they got a truly 'adult' reply!

WHAT HAPPENS IN INTERACTIONS WITH OTHERS?

If you are reading about Transactional Analysis for the first time, you may be thinking this is very straightforward: if we all know what Parent, Adult and Child behaviour is like and can describe it, how is it that we end up in unhelpful exchanges with other people?

That takes us back to the 'hardwiring' and so the habits we have formed, as well as the small matter of where we are placing our attention…

Eric Berne described the normal exchanges we have with others as **'Complementary'** transactions, usually illustrated like this:

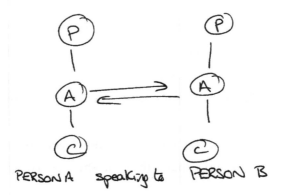

Adult-Adult

When we ask another person an 'adult' question we normally get an 'adult' response. Our words, demeanour and voice tone 'hooks' an adult response in them. E.g. 'What time is the meeting?' gets the reply '11.30'

Parent-Child

If on the other hand, we use a Controlling Parent ego state we are likely to hook a Child response, either Rebellious or Conforming depending on who the 'Child' is and the relationship between the two. Eg 'I don't think you should be at that meeting!' gets the rebellious reply 'That's none of your business!'

Child-Parent

Similarly, if we speak to someone in a Child ego state we will likely hook a Parental response. This could be any part of the Child (Rebellious, Conforming or Free) and once again depending on who is involved and their relationship, the response may come from the Controlling or Nurturing Parent. E.g. 'I'm not going to bother to prepare for that meeting. No-one else does!' gets the reply 'I think you should consider how that reflects on this department!'

Child-Child

Some child behaviour will 'hook' a child response in others. E.g. Rebellious: 'Let's just not turn up at the meeting and see what they do about it!' gets the response 'Yes it will serve them right if they have to wait, they might be a bit more appreciative of us next time!'

Conforming: 'I think I will just keep my head down in this meeting, I cannot stand the arguments' gets the reply 'Me too!'

Free: 'Right, I'm off to the pub!!' gets the reply 'I'll come with you… just to keep you company of course!'

Sometimes, of course, we take other people up wrongly or vice versa and then we could say we have our wires crossed. What Eric Berne called 'Crossed' transactions. They look like this:

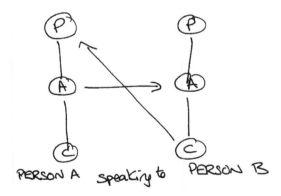

PERSON A speaking to PERSON B

This happens when for example Person A's Adult question is heard differently by Person B. It may sound Parental to them and hence they come back with a Child response. For example: 'If you are going out for a sandwich can you get me one?' gets the reply ' No! Get it yourself!' This may well be met with the internal response in Person A 'Aargh… why are they talking to me like this?'

The feeling may be confusion, and perhaps anger at the response, which may, in turn, provoke Person A to come back with a Parental riposte. What ensues can be an argument or bad feeling between the two. Person A's behaviour is in effect being controlled by Person B.

So why does this happen and what can we do about it? There can be a myriad of reasons why someone might hear an Adult remark or question as Parent or Child. It may be that Person B is stressed about something at home or work, they could be in a hurry or even just argued with someone else. It is also possible of course that Person A's past behaviour is the influencing factor here. If the relationship matters, wouldn't it be good if Person A applied more choice to their response rather than letting the hardwiring take over?

IS THERE A PLACE FOR 'PARENT' AND 'CHILD' BEHAVIOUR IN WORK ENVIRONMENTS?

In a word: Yes! There are a number of situations when being in the Parent ego state is not just tolerated, but even looked for. In an emergency, or facing a tight deadline, for example, it can be comforting to others to have someone take control. On the other hand, there are times when the compassionate approach of the Nurturing Parent may be just what someone needs. Notice that these are to some degree 'exceptional' events and so when used more widely the effect can be destructive.

Often when we go into a 'Parent' ego state our intentions are sound, we want to help, guide or keep another person safe. The other person, however, may not recognise our well-meaning motives and instead feel demeaned, patronised or even bullied. And of course that then 'hooks' a child response in them... which we in turn find may antagonistic or irritating.

Similarly, there are times when especially the Free Child is both welcome and useful. Used appropriately, humour and a sense of fun are essential to our well-being and quality of life and having a bonding effect with friends and colleagues. If we use it without consideration of others around us then the effect is crass and even disruptive.

What about the Adapted Child? Is there a place for our rebellious-ness or compliance? Particularly in our work environments, it is harder to make a case for the effective use of these behaviours. Both run the risk of us being dismissed as childish and a good point expressed in a rebellious way is often lost. Within an organisation, most people accept 'the chain of command' and recognise that their boss has the right and responsibility to make the final decision on a work issue. If we do this in a compliant way i.e. Conforming Child, this can be frustrating to others, who are not sure what we really think. When we do this in an Adult way, we may have expressed our point and so there are less likely to be doubts and tension.

RESISTING THE 'HARDWIRING' AND MOVING THE 'MIRROR'

When it comes to resisting the hardwiring the issue is our attention and where it is focussed. When we are in conversation with others our attention may be on how they are behaving, without much consideration of what our part in it is. While our focus is on them and judging their response, we are not taking any responsibility for what may be going wrong. We are back at the wrong end of the cause > effect equation referred to in Chapter 1.

Frank Pucelik (one of the original co-founders of NLP) summarised the problem this way in his session at the NLP International Conference in May 2017:

When we have an interaction with another person, we interpret what they say through our own 'map of the world'

So when we respond, we are looking in our own 'mirror' and judging that person from our own experiences, standards and reactions. We are not really looking at them or how it is for them.

Frank concludes "Until you can move the 'mirror' you cannot be a professional communicator."

So to have a positive impact in our relationships with others we need to move our own 'mirror' and start to consider how it is for them. This thinking alone takes us into Adult territory. A useful question when puzzled by another's behaviour is:

What has to be true for them for this behaviour to be logical or understandable?

At the start of this chapter, I said that as far as we can tell, most people consider themselves sane and their behaviour in the moment is logical. If we could take ourselves to the point of understanding: 'What has to be true for them?' we may be better able to stay in a calm, resourceful place with them and achieve a better outcome.

I was running a 2-day course with a group that I hadn't worked with before. It was clear from mutterings over the pre-course coffee that there were 'issues' back in their department which were causing bad feeling. Not the best start to any course! As I went around the group asking what they wanted to get from the training, one response came back "I WANT YOU TO DO MAGIC!"… more accurately, spat back! In my 'map of the world' that was more than a little rude and yet to react the way my hardwiring might dictate, would have made working with that person, let alone the group, very difficult. Instead, I swiftly concluded that this wasn't 'about me', (way too early in the course to hate me I thought!), and instead assured her that we would be getting on to 'magic' later in the morning. Her reaction was confusion mixed with surprise, (a crossed transaction, you might say), nonetheless, the more general reaction in the group was humour and relief… and so we were able to usefully carry on.

I later found out that the group had been told prior to the course that redundancies were likely. The point is that I didn't know that at the time, but it is a useful 'default' position to stay in the

Adult, not make assumptions, or be too judgemental about another person's behaviour.

HOOKING ADULT BEHAVIOUR IN OTHERS

The really great thing about staying in the Adult ego state is that it takes a lot less work than you might think because as I have said already, responding to 'adult' with 'adult' behaviour is hardwired too. When we speak to someone in a way that is respectful of ourselves as well as them, it is most likely to get an Adult response in the moment, or sometimes (if their emotions have been high), when they calm down and reflect on it.

This is because, particularly in emotional situations, we are not fuelling the negative emotion: being listened to and responded to in a calm respectful way usually has the effect of neutralising anger.

It can often feel though that it is not our fault, or indeed that the situation or the behaviour of others, is not in our immediate control. Yet it is good to recognise that there is always choice and at least something we can do to impact on a situation for the better. Consider Jack Canfield's often quoted formula:

$$E + R = O$$

Event/Experience + Our Reaction = Outcome

The 'event or the experience' can be something over which we have little control in the short term. It may be the organisation you work for, your boss, your colleagues, central government policy, the weather or even a health issue. None of these in themselves create the 'outcome'; the key variable is how we choose to react. (Doing nothing is also a choice!)

So it is *our reaction* that really determines the outcome... which puts us back in a more powerful place, and in effect back at Cause.

An example of this is Jane Tomlinson. Jane was an amateur athlete who was diagnosed with terminal cancer in 2000 and given 12 months to live. Her reaction was to take on a series of gruelling challenges (marathons, triathlons etc) and raised £1.85m for cancer charities. Jane died in 2007 and the fundraising carries on in her name. At the time of writing the amount raised topped £10m. So she changed the outcome for herself, her family and the many who will benefit from the funds she raised.

There are numerous examples of others who have experienced great good fortune in their lives and their reaction has been to squander it and end up losing fortunes, family and friends.

So we can make a great impact for ourselves and others when we *choose* our reaction... and hence our impact. In the next chapter, I will explore some resourceful 'attitudes/beliefs' that can help us to do just that.

Exercise:

Take some time to consider some of the interactions you have had with others where you weren't happy with the outcome... and think about your answers to these questions:

- What 'ego' state were you and the other person(s) in?
- What effect were you having on each other?
- What learning is there for you in this? Have you spotted an unhelpful pattern in your own behaviour?
- How else could you have reacted that might have changed/improved the outcome?

KEY POINTS:

» Wilder Penfield and Eric Berne proposed that the human brain records every life event and feeling and these go to making up our personality

» The 'normal' human personality is made up of Parent, Adult and Child ego states and all of these emerge many times through a typical day and even within a conversation

» Our reactions are hardwired from early in life. If someone speaks in a parental tone it is likely to elicit a child response, similarly someone speaking or behaving in the child ego state will most likely hook a parental response

» Fortunately, if we speak to someone from our adult ego state we are likely to elicit an adult response. So when we put ourselves at Cause, we can choose our response to situations rather than giving in to the hardwiring

» Frank Pucelik says that "unless you can move the mirror you cannot be a professional communicator"

» Event/Experience + Our Reaction = Outcome

Chapter 4

So How Can I Get My Head and Heart Right?

WHEN KNOWING IT ISN'T ENOUGH

In the last chapter, I looked at behaviour using the theory of Transactional Analysis. Whether you have come across that theory before or not, I was probably telling you something that you already knew at some level.

We do not always give forethought to our words or actions, yet on reflection, if we had, the reaction we get from others could have been anticipated. Knowing this, we can still find ourselves handling conversations with others in ways that don't work for us or for the relationship. In this chapter, I explore how we can get head and heart working together to achieve the outcomes we want. So let's start by looking at what is driving our behaviour.

THE LOGICAL LEVELS OF BEHAVIOUR

A valuable model from NLP which describes the process is Robert Dilts' Logical Levels of Behaviour model (sometimes referred to as Neuro-Logical Levels), which I think is most easily explained when shown as an iceberg:

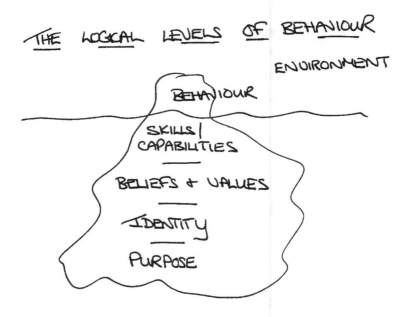

Humans have things in common with icebergs. We often say that behaviour is 'the tip of the iceberg' suggesting that there is a great deal more driving their behaviour, to that which we see on the surface. Our behaviour is not just supported by what is 'under the waterline', it is impacted by the environment that we are in and is to some degree a reaction to it. (It is almost a daily news item now how global warming in our environment is affecting the polar ice and the icebergs that break away from it.)

To explain the model further let's look at someone who is performing well in the job i.e. their behaviour is effective:

Environment: this gives their behaviour context and it is more often the case that when someone is performing well, there is something happening in their environment that supports that performance such as their line manager, their team or other resources.

Behaviour: this is what we can actually observe i.e. what someone is doing and saying and it is this observable evidence that would lead us to conclude that they are effective.

Skills/Capabilities: their ability to do this is in turn enabled by the skills and capabilities they possess. This could be innate or as a result of their education or experience. This is a direct support to their effective behaviour.

Beliefs/Values: many people have skills and knowledge that they do not use e.g. someone who has passed their driving test may not choose to drive. Another example that you may have experienced in the workplace is a colleague who has great experience and job knowledge but may come to you or others for reassurance on their decisions. The issue here is not just what they know, but what they believe about themselves, the dangers on the road or the perils of making a mistake. So for someone to use the skills and knowledge they have, they have to believe in their own ability and the value of the task to be carried out. So this level, in turn, supports their skills and capabilities and allows the person to use these to the full.

Identity: some beliefs are held at identity level i.e. how we see and describe ourselves. For an individual performing well in their role, that role is likely to be a key part of how they see themselves e.g. they may say: I am a leader or I am a parent. 'I am…' statements are indicators of Identity, be they positive or negative statements. How they see themselves supports their beliefs about themselves and what they place value on.

Purpose: (This is sometimes also described as Mission or Spirit.) This is the deepest level of all, what we are all about as a person. For someone to perform at their best, their role must fit with this level and help to achieve it. Typical examples of how someone might see their purpose is 'to be happy' or to 'look after my family'. So this level supports/drives all the rest.

When all of these levels are consistent with one another, then we present ourselves, and indeed behave, in a way that is congruent and authentic. It is us at our best.

So in summary, what we believe about ourselves, other people or a situation is what determines our behaviour, far more than our skills and what we know. An example of this is someone asked to complete a task at work. Sometime later their manager may notice it is not done and ask why. When the reply comes back "I haven't had time", that is probably not an indicator of what they are *able* to do, but more likely an indicator of the priority they have given the task i.e. what they *believe* about the task they have been asked to complete. It could also in some cases be an indicator of how they feel about their own ability to complete it. Either way, what is driving their behaviour is what they believe about the task, themselves or maybe even their manager.

So for us to really achieve the outcomes we want, it is not enough to just 'know what to do'…

- we have to believe in our ability to do it
- we may need to hold more resourceful beliefs about others
- and we need to place real value on those outcomes.

We need to get our head and heart 'right'!

PRE-SUPPOSITIONS OF NLP – RESOURCEFUL BELIEFS

So what do I mean about getting our 'head and heart right'? In short, it is about getting our whole selves to buy into what we are looking to achieve.

Consider this for a moment:

When you have made a good decision … how do you know? What tells you? Is it just your head knowing it is logical, or do you have any other feelings or sensations in your body that tell you it's right?

Most people report feeling something in their 'heart' or in their 'gut' when they have made a good (or a bad decision), so our assessment has a somatic, (i.e. felt in the body), element as well as a mental one.

We really feel it when we know we are doing or saying something that is right (or wrong of course). So what kind of thinking will help us get our 'head, heart… and gut right'?

In her book "The Bumper Book of Modelling" Fran Burgess describes the pre-suppositions as some of the key thinking that underpins NLP. These pre-suppositions come from a variety of sources which can be summarised, I think, as beliefs of excellence or more simply attitudes that work.

When we choose to take these beliefs or attitudes on board, the result is more resourceful behaviour and a greater likelihood of achieving our outcomes. So let's look at some of these beliefs. As you read them, consider what taking these on as an approach might give you in your relationships… maybe how you see yourself… and indeed what they could enable you to do:

Everyone has a different map of the world: in Chapter 2 I referred to Constructivism as a key theory also underpinning NLP i.e. our individual 'map of the world' and how we see it is built from our experiences. When we take this belief on board we are to some degree *expecting* other people to see things differently from us, AND *respecting* the way they see it, whether we agree with them or not. When we start from this premise, it impacts the way in which we present ourselves to others in terms of our body language and voice tone. This approach is, therefore, more likely to promote dialogue and agreement.

The map is not the territory: in this pre-supposition, there is the useful recognition that how we see it is not necessarily how it is. Just taking out the certainty that 'we are right' transforms how we assess a situation or another's motives. We may be more curious and we may listen better to others.

The person with the most flexibility has the greatest influence: there is an expression 'every problem is a nail if all you have got is a hammer'. Put like that it is apparent how limiting it is when we are inflexible in our approach and when we expect others to understand us, rather than seek to make ourselves understood.

Structures we see in others mirrors structures we see in ourselves: perhaps a more direct way to think of this is 'everyone you meet is a mirror'. What we like or dislike in others reminds us of something in ourselves. Taking this on as an idea can be a big learning opportunity and even get us into the 'Blind Area' that I mentioned when looking at Johari Window in Chapter 1. 'What is my reaction to another person's behaviour teaching me about myself... and what do I need to be working on?' The answer to that, in turn, is likely to make us less judgemental of others as well as more aware of ourselves and our impact.

We cannot not communicate / The meaning of a communication is the message that is understood: I have put both of these together because firstly everything we say and do communicates something to other people whether we intended to or not. And secondly, whilst their interpretation may not be correct, it is to true for them, and they will respond to it based on that. So we need to be alert to the messages we are giving others, and respectful of how they receive it. Then in this way our communications with others are likely to be smoother.

There is no failure only feedback: many people carry a fear of failure and getting it wrong, so much so that it acts as an inhibitor. When things do not go as we planned, it is more useful to look at what we learned from the experience than label it as failure and potentially learn nothing but avoidance. This pre-supposition might also shift how we give feedback to others as well as ourselves.

People make the best choices available to them at the time: in the last chapter I pointed out that most people consider themselves sane and when we act in the moment it might seem like the right thing to do, whatever we conclude later on. It is the same for other people too. We may not like their behaviour, but when we consider that they might see this as their best choice at the time, we might accord them the same understanding that we give ourselves.

Behind every action is an (unconscious) positive intention: this is perhaps one of the more challenging pre-suppositions to take on board. The more challenging, however, is likely to mean the one that will bring the greatest change in our own behaviour! There is obviously a 'reason' behind everyone's behaviour that in some way is positive to them. That may be misguided of course, but seeing it as 'their issue' may stop us from taking the behaviour of others personally and keep us in a calmer, more resourceful place.

If something isn't working do something different: Einstein is credited with saying "The definition of insanity is doing the same thing over and over again, but expecting different results". It's worth considering do we repeat behaviours that do not serve us?

We all have all the resources we need: this is a resourceful belief that we can hold about ourselves and others. When we do, it is less likely that we underestimate other people or ourselves. So it gives a powerful positive message to people around us and also to ourselves. Once again holding this belief transforms how we present ourselves and therefore the reactions we get.

The mind and the body are part of the same system: in Chapter 2, I introduced the NLP Communication model which illustrates exactly this, i.e. what is going on on the inside, will be showing on the outside and therefore giving a message to others. When we recognise the logic of this, it really emphasises the need to get our head and heart right!

Memory and imagination are wired on the same circuits: this idea that if you imagine yourself being successful your chances of actual success are greatly increased is one espoused by sports people of all types and in Chapter 6 I talk about one in particular, Muhammed Ali. This idea is developed by Dr Maxwell Maltz in his book "Psycho-Cybernetics", he said:

"Human beings always act and feel and perform in accordance with what they imagine to be true about themselves and their environment."

ARE THE PRE-SUPPOSITIONS OF NLP TRUE... DOES IT MATTER?

This is a question I often hear when I discuss the pre-suppositions and my reply is 'Does it matter?'

Buddha is quoted as saying:

> *"Believe nothing, no matter where you read it, or who said it, no matter if I have said it unless it agrees with your own reason and your own common sense."*

Rather than debate whether the pre-suppositions are true or not, it is usually more useful to consider what happens when we behave *'as if'* they are true. Their power is in what they enable us to do: the ability to stay calm, ask questions, listen to others. They allow us to manage our state and stay in a resourceful place to handle what is happening in the moment. They allow our heart and gut to work in harmony with our head rather than be in internal turmoil.

John Grinder (one of the original co-founders of NLP) pointed to this when said there are three barriers to effectiveness:

- Muscle tension
- Foveal vision
- Inner Chatter

When we get into an unresourceful state such as anger, we experience these very things. Our muscles tense up, we focus on 'one thing' (rather than take a broader view) and we experience this chatter or debate in our head. Unsurprisingly this doesn't enable us to be at our best or take the wisest course. Taking on the pre-suppositions as an 'attitude' or perhaps even better as a belief, allows us to manage our state and dismantle these barriers. Now …that <u>does</u> matter!

WILL THE PRE-SUPPOSITIONS MAKE ME INTO POLLYANNA?

Taken from the eponymous hero of Eleanor H. Porter's novel, there is something called the 'Pollyanna principle' which describes the tendency of the unconscious to focus on the positive, particularly when looking back over past events. The conscious mind it seems has a tendency to focus on the negative. So perhaps it is this that makes some people rather concerned that embracing the pre-suppositions is unrealistic or even would make them vulnerable in some way.

A delegate on a course with me once exclaimed: "But Florence there IS failure, it exists!!" I wholeheartedly agreed with him, it does, and then pointed out that the value of taking the attitude that *'there is no failure only feedback'*, is in how you react to that failure, what you learn from it and how you approach it with others. This is not a denial of failure; it is about how do you usefully and resourcefully move on from it.

Similarly, I hear concerns that a number of the pre-suppositions, when applied to other people's behaviour, could suggest that in some way their behaviour is not just understandable but acceptable.

This is not the case either. If you are someone's line manager, for example, you have both the responsibility to ensure that work is carried out satisfactorily and the right to say how that should be done. The value of taking the attitude *'people make the best choices available to them at the time'*, particularly if something has gone wrong, is the state it creates in you. Once again in allowing you to be calm and clear when speaking to your team member, this increases the likelihood of a useful dialogue between you, and an acceptance of feedback.

So, far from playing the Pollyanna 'Glad Game', (something to be glad about in every situation), embracing the pre-suppositions are much more about taking a broader view, staying alert to a range of possibilities and creating more resourceful states in us.

To quote Psychologist Stephen Gilligan PhD:

> *"The outcomes a person produces are*
> *only as good as the state they are in"*

SO WHAT IMPACT DO MY BELIEFS HAVE ON OTHERS AND MYSELF?

In Chapter 2, I described the NLP Communication Model and followed the implications of our thinking right through to the effect on our physiology and then on to what shows on the outside i.e. how we look, how we sound and what we say. All of these, in turn, are observed and interpreted by other people – our thinking and our beliefs quickly start to impact on others, often in ways that we did not intend.

In Chapter 3, I described the 'hard-wiring' we have since child-hood. So when we think we are being spoken to in *parental* way our impulse, (if we go with the hardwiring), is to reply in a *child* ego state, with all the consequences of this on the relationship. Instead by managing our state, i.e. by embracing the pre-suppositions, we can resist the hard-wiring and choose our response in a situation. In this way, we can keep conversations in an 'adult' place and indeed 'hook' an adult response from others.

Another concern I have heard about managing our state in this way is summed up in a fabulous phrase I heard from a delegate at the start of the course – he was concerned the effect of the course would be to plunge him into *'an abyss of neutrality'*. It is a phrase (unsurprisingly) that has stuck with me and he and I have laughed about it (with him) since. Because what he came to realise was that managing your state is not about being 'neutral': it is about being able to express your views in a way that is respectful of yourself and others, whilst staying attentive to the whole conversation. When we do this, of course, there is every danger they might just be interested in what we have to say!

The pre-suppositions are not just about our relationships with others, possibly more fundamentally they impact on how we think of, and therefore how we present ourselves.

The impact of our beliefs about ourselves can be summed up by the belief cycle:

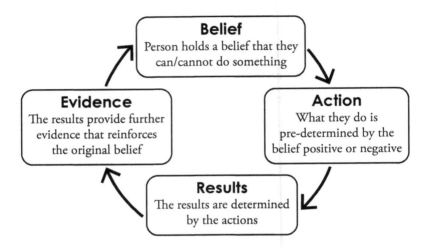

Put simply our beliefs are a self-fulfilling prophecy. There may be a number of situations or relationships that challenge us, about which we may be holding limiting beliefs. As the model below shows it is likely therefore that we are holding ourselves in this negative belief cycle. You may recognise the link here with Cognitive Behavioural Therapy. CBT is based on the concept that how we think and feel and what we do are interconnected, and so negative beliefs can trap you in a vicious cycle.

On the other hand, we can *choose* to make a change and break out of this, by using the technique of behaving 'as if'. Here is how it works applied to chairing a meeting: let's start with the negative belief that 'I am not good enough to run this meeting effectively':

Negative Belief Cycle:

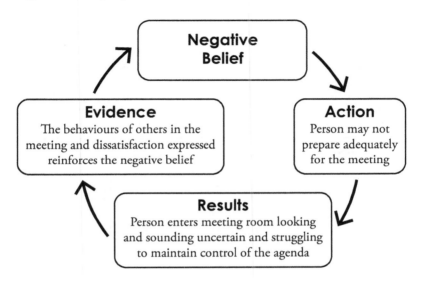

Negative Belief

Evidence
The behaviours of others in the meeting and dissatisfaction expressed reinforces the negative belief

Action
Person may not prepare adequately for the meeting

Results
Person enters meeting room looking and sounding uncertain and struggling to maintain control of the agenda

Positive Belief Cycle – Behaving 'As If'

In the diagram overleaf, the positive belief cycle is 'I am capable of running the meeting effectively when well prepared':

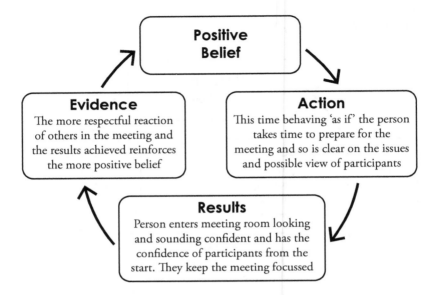

So behaving 'as if' is the start of shifting limiting beliefs we may be holding and it is simply a stage in the process. When we start to get evidence that supports a more resourceful belief, we are no longer behaving 'as if', we are really starting to believe it.

In Chapter 2 I talked about the power of the unconscious mind and in Chapter 7 I will expand on this by looking at some of the duties and characteristics of the unconscious. One of these is that the unconscious is literal in its interpretation and looks to prove us right, so whatever we choose to believe, positive or negative, about ourselves or others, the unconscious mind will find the evidence to support it! So the choice is ours, how we want to see ourselves, how we want to be seen by others and how we want to relate to others. After all *'the person with the most flexibility has the greatest influence'*.

In the words of Henry Ford (founder of the Ford Motor Company):

"Whether you think you can or you think you cannot – you're right"

Exercise

Take this opportunity to 'try on' some of the pre-suppositions (much in the way that you might do with an item of clothing before buying!).

Think about a situation where you would like to present yourself in a more effective 'adult' state, and then, which of the pre-suppositions would help you to do that?

It may be a more resourceful belief about yourself or another person in the situation. Then consider each of these questions in turn. It may be helpful to write down your answers to each or physically step forward as you consider each question – both of these will allow you to take an active part in the process. Even better get someone else to ask you the questions:

When you believe XXX

Environment: Describe what your environment will be like ...

Behaviour: Describe what you will be doing differently... how you are sitting/moving/speaking/eye contact etc

Skills/Capabilities: What skills are you now able to fully use (that maybe you haven't up till now)?

Beliefs/Values: *Notice what it is like to believe* XXX *(about yourself/others)? What is important to you about believing* XXX?

Identity: *When you believe* XXX *how does this enhance how you see yourself?*

Purpose: *How does believing* XXX *fit with what you are about as a person and your future?*

Knowing all of this now, what actions are you committing to taking going forward?

KEY POINTS:

» Our behaviour is driven more by our beliefs and values than our skills and capabilities

» For us to achieve the outcomes we want, we need to hold resourceful beliefs about ourselves and place value on the outcome

» When we make judgements about a decision, for example, we feel it in both our cognitive mind and in our somatic mind

» The pre-suppositions are a key underpinning element of NLP and are resourceful beliefs and attitudes that can enable us to reframe our approach to ourselves and others.

» Whether they are true or not, their power is in behaving 'as if' they are true

» The unconscious has a tendency to look back positively whilst the conscious mind has a negativity bias – the pre-suppositions are about putting/keeping us in a resourceful state

» We can programme ourselves for a successful (or unsuccessful) outcome

Chapter 5
Staying On Track... How am I Doing?

HOW DO WE KNOW OUR SHIFTS IN THINKING AND BEHAVIOUR ARE WORKING?

Nowhere is the gulf between intention and impact more apparent, than when it comes to giving and receiving feedback. Whatever our intention, our impact on others is not always clear... or at least it isn't if we ignore it. That could mean not paying attention to the reactions from others, to the feedback they are giving us, (in whatever form), or if we do not actively seek their feedback. In Chapter 1, I referred to both the 'risk' we might feel in asking others for feedback, and the fact that without it, we get stuck in our 'Blind Area', not knowing our impact on others, good or bad.

Sometimes people actively avoid feedback from others… and when we do this, we are actively choosing to stay in our 'Blind Area', potentially not making adjustments to improve things and not having the full satisfaction of our successes either.

In this Chapter, I will focus on the effect of feedback on us and others that can go unrecognised, and how we can give and receive feedback to improve:

- our performance,
- our self-esteem
- and enrich our relationships with others.

CAN I GIVE YOU SOME FEEDBACK?

The short question 'Can I give you some feedback?' has such an association for many people that according to neuroscientist Dr David Rock it creates a feeling of dread and fear similar to the feeling of someone walking behind us on a dark night!

The reason for this response may be previous experiences, as well as the fact that the brain has a strong 'negativity bias' in how it processes those experiences. In a scientific paper titled 'Bad Is Stronger Than Good' Roy Baumeister and his colleagues pointed to how the brain looks for negative information and over-reacts to it. As a result, negative conversations have more impact on a relationship than positive ones. This pre-disposition to look for snags and pitfalls is a useful survival strategy for Stone Age man, less useful in modern life and relationships… and for giving balanced useful feedback!

It is worth noting it is not just other people who may be drawn to giving us feedback in this way, (even if their intention in doing so is a good one): as Timothy Gallwey states in his book "The Inner Game of Tennis", we have an internal critic also whose unhelpful observations promote self-doubt and hesitation creating *'interference'*. His well-known formula sums it up beautifully:

"Potential minus interference equals performance."

What could we do better when we get out of our own way, and match our good intention to the impact we want to make?

GIVING FEEDBACK THAT 'PEOPLE CAN HEAR'

So how can feedback be more useful, what I refer to as feedback that 'people can hear'? Sometimes the way feedback is given, regardless of its intention, sparks a defensive response and the receiver is unable to really 'hear' what is being said.

On training courses when I talk about giving feedback, the first reaction often reflects a 'negativity bias'. A typical reaction when I ask delegates to give feedback to one another is dread. Then when I suggest giving people at work more balanced feedback, delegates behave as if I am speaking from 'The Mother Teresa School of Management' – (my term), meaning that this all seems a bit 'soft' in some way. The format for the balanced feedback I am encouraging them to use is:

- To start with: *'I liked/appreciated...*
- And if there is something you would like the person to do differently then give: *'An improver'* – this is expressed in a positive way e.g. a suggestion or guidance rather than saying what 'I didn't like xxx'

Initially, there is often still an air of scepticism in the room until I start to talk about the effect of feedback on the brain, and it is at that point that people 'get it'.

Far from being the 'soft' approach, there are a number of studies that show that when people experience positive emotions, like when they are hearing positive feedback, their stress levels are lower and it promotes effectiveness. Daniel Goleman in his book "Social Intelligence: The New Science of Human Relationships" points out that brain activity associated with positive emotions enhances mental abilities such as *"creative thinking, cognitive flexibility, and the processing of information"* – not surprising really when research quoted by Noelle Nelson PhD shows that blood flow also increases to the brain when they receive positive feedback.

Put simply when we give people positive, specific, verifiable feedback, this enables them to think better and apply the feedback across a range of situations. As you might expect, it also has an effect on their confidence and self-esteem. Like any other mental capability, inner strengths are supported by structures in the brain. Through what's called 'experience-dependent neuroplasticity' the more often people experience these positive feelings about themselves the more they develop strong neural networks that support inner strengths.

Given the 'negativity bias' of the human brain, to encourage these neural traits we need to hear more positives than negatives and indeed Nancy Kline in her Book "Time to Think" suggests a ratio of 5:1!

WHAT HAPPENS WHEN SOMEONE'S BEHAVIOUR OR PERFORMANCE IS UNSATISFACTORY?

Sometimes a person's behaviour is not effective and we want to encourage change. Helping them to see this and influence a change is where the idea of giving this feedback as 'an Improver' comes in. Often this is when feedback becomes a negative and the way this is communicated can feel like a threat to the brain prompting a 'flight or fight' response. In this case, the person is not focussed on their own behaviour but on that of the giver... and defending themselves of course. When giving 'an Improver', rather than saying " I didn't like..." or "Don't ...", instead tell or suggest to the person what you think they could do differently. This feels different to both the giver and the receiver... and gets to the point. When we start by telling someone what we didn't like or what we don't want them to do, it is confusing, and we can end up reinforcing the very behaviour we want to change. In Chapter 7, I will make further reference to the unconscious mind and one of the most easily demonstrated of the characteristics of the unconscious is that it cannot process a negative. For example, if I say "Don't think about Judy Garland" notice what comes to mind, we have to create Judy Garland first before attempting to not think about her. So if I say to someone "Don't be late for that meeting tomorrow" what the brain hears is 'be late'. It is more useful as an Improver to say what I want instead "Be on time for that meeting tomorrow".

When I was explaining this on one occasion a course delegate exclaimed: "Oh I just call that giving guidance!" Done respectfully giving an 'Improver', as opposed to a criticism, is more likely to get a positive outcome and even feel more like a collaborative discussion than the feedback people often fear.

Surely the whole point in giving feedback, whether it is in a work setting or in a personal relationship, is to be heard and to enable the person concerned to be able to make a change. In this case, it is not a 'soft' option to give it in this way. It is a more logical and effective choice.

WHAT ABOUT RECEIVING FEEDBACK?

In managing our impact on others we can give feedback in this way, but when it comes to receiving feedback from others, even complimentary feedback can be difficult to accept... and the feed-back from others may not be given so thoughtfully!

Some people feel a level of embarrassment when given complimentary feedback, (they may not be used to it!), and their response is often to diminish it in some way, in effect to reject it. Whilst this display of modesty might be cute in some way, the brain of the giver also interprets this 'rejection' as a threat, you may see the giver move back slightly, and the likelihood of them giving feedback in the future to you is reduced. So to keep the feedback flowing just say 'Thank you!' ... or ask for clarification if you need it. Batting it away or justifying yourself is a sure way of staying in the dark.

When we get feedback from others they may not be so careful about how they give it. They may genuinely think, (like some people whom I have worked with in the past), that telling you where you are going wrong is the best way to help. Even in this circumstance, we can move from 'effect' to 'cause' by also asking them what they are pleased with, or what they think is going well. This has the additional effect of directing their attention too and creating more balance in their minds about us. Nancy Kline says that our minds work best in the presence of reality, and the reality for all of us, I think, is that there are things we do well and things we could do better.

Perhaps best of all when we actually ask for feedback and then really listen to it, we are showing huge trust in the giver; particularly when we ask more questions to understand it rather than attempt to justify ourselves. In that situation, we put the giver more at ease and more likely to give feedback freely to us in the future.

IS THERE ANYTHING ELSE TO REMEMBER ABOUT GIVING FEEDBACK?

I have written so far about the concerns that we may feel about receiving feedback and how to give it effectively. I think it is important to acknowledge though that it can be equally difficult for some people to give feedback, so much so, that often people simply don't, often with unfortunate consequences.

At an earlier stage in my career, I worked in an H.R. role. I received a phone call on one occasion from a manager that went like this:

Me: "How can I help you?"

Manager: "I want to sack my supervisor!"

Me: "For what reason?"

Manager: "Because she is c**p!"

Me: "Oh…I think we are going to need a bit more information on that. What is the problem?"

Manager: "She is rude to me and customers"

Me: "How long has she worked for you?

Manager: "Six years"

Me: "How long has she been behaving like that?"

Manager: "Six years"

Me: "Have you given her any feedback about her behaviour?"

Manager: "Well no… she is very touchy you know…very hard to talk to…"

Me: "So she has been rude to you and customers for six years and you have said nothing to her about it… it is not going to be very fair to sack her then is it?"

Manager: "Well…not when you put it like that!"

So the first thing is to actually GIVE feedback. It is probable that this supervisor was subjected to dark looks and oblique remarks by her manager. In which case, the manager's impact was not the corrective one she intended, more likely the supervisor saw her manager's behaviour as rude and passive-aggressive.

Another pitfall is to give 'blanket' feedback; this can be equally unhelpful and misleading and can sound insincere. For some people, to tell them "You are really great at presenting" can be translated through their filters as: "You are perfect at presenting", so they may reject any future 'Improvers' you suggest. To others, it may just seem like old flannel. It's a good guide to think 'What will the person learn from my feedback?'

THE PYGMALION EFFECT

The most reliable way to see more of behaviour you want from someone is to point it out to them. It is an exciting thought that your feedback can help others grow in skill and confidence – this has become known as the 'Pygmalion Effect' named after George Bernard Shaw's play of that name, where the professor transforms the flower seller Eliza. Rosenthal and Jacobson in their book "Pygmalion In The Classroom" describe this phenomenon that the expectations we express of others make it more likely that they will behave in that way.

This can work the other way too when feedback is overly critical and the individual meets the lowered expectations of them. An example of this might be a child who is frequently misbehaving being told off in front of the class: the result is often to see more of that bad behaviour, not less!

FEEDBACK BECOMING A CULTURE

Feedback can and does become part of the culture in a team or an organisation. In my experience the effect of this is transformational.

Earlier in my career, I was part of a training team that was composed of some of the most talented people I have met. At first, I didn't recognise my good fortune because we were dysfunctional, to say the least... then we got a new manager.

At our first team meeting with her, I had a squabble with another colleague… (and we were the training team remember!) After that meeting, I complained to my manager saying "Did you hear how xxx spoke to me in that meeting?" she replied that she had and I retorted "Well are you going to speak to him about it?" Her reply was "No I am not…have you given him that feedback?" And so we began to give each other feedback, which eventually grew into encouraging and acknowledging the great work that was being produced. As a team, both in our relationships and our productivity we were transformed. Perhaps more interesting still is that decades later most of that team are still in regular contact with one another.

And that person I had the squabble with? I get his feedback every time he gets my newsletter, and I value it.

A friend was telling me about a pub he visited on holiday in Ireland. The barman's opening line to each new customer was "Talk to me!" – Now there was a man who knew something about the essence of effective relationships.

Exercise:

As you read through this chapter you may already have thought about friends or colleagues to where your feedback could have a positive impact, or areas of your life and work where you could do with more feedback.

- So now think about how you could best deliver that feedback to help and encourage that person(s). And as you do, you might reflect on a pre-supposition from the last chapter 'Structures we see in others mirrors structures we see in ourselves' and consider 'what has my observations of them got to teach me about myself?'
- Also, think about who could give you feedback on the areas where you want to develop?

KEY POINTS:

» Getting feedback can feel like a risk but without it, we risk staying in ignorance in our 'Blind Area'

» Humans have a strong negativity bias which makes us apprehensive about feedback

» Positive feedback impacts in a beneficial way on our effectiveness and stress levels and increases blood flow to the brain

» Giving feedback on behaviour that needs to change in some way can be done effectively as an 'Improver' i.e. what you want rather than what you didn't like

» Receiving feedback – just say 'thank you' – how they see it is how it is for them

» There is a danger in not giving feedback as it leaves the impression that the behaviour, good or bad, doesn't matter or is acceptable in some way

» The Pygmalion effect of feedback – we are likely to see more of behaviour that is praised

Chapter 6
Ooops... Did I Just Say That?

ARE LANGUAGE AND SUCCESS LINKED?

What it is that makes successful people successful? Numerous books have been written on the subject and people continue to be fascinated by this question. There is something enabling them to achieve success in the first place and helping them to recover from setbacks and perhaps criticism from others along the way. There is also something special about how they connect with people and how they make them feel... their impact on others you might say.

Whilst it is unsafe to generalise, it is not always because they are the best at what they do, or because they had the best educational opportunities, or even that they were born into wealthy families. Whatever they have, a common trait is their drive to succeed and positivity. I am curious about how these are linked. This positivity shows not just in actions but in language – something about how they speak that tells us how they think and perhaps what they believe about themselves.

I remember watching a well-known football team captain being interviewed before a big match. His head was down, he was hunched over, his voice tone was dull and his comment about the match was: "It will be a disaster for us if we lose this match." They lost.

It is too great a stretch to presume that if he had been more upbeat they would have won. Still, I can't help thinking it may have made a difference. In contrast to that, Martin Luther King's 'I have a dream speech' delivered in 1963 is still uplifting to hear or read more than 50 years on. If you haven't ever read it in full I urge you to do so, to feel the power of the language. Here is a short extract that may give you a feel for it:

"With this faith, we will be able to hew out
of the mountain of despair a stone of hope.
With this faith, we will be able to trans-
form the jangling discords of our nation into
a beautiful symphony of brotherhood"

Language has a way of influencing us, as just about everything we say pre-supposes something. Take a look at the title of this section – it poses the question: 'Are Language and Success Linked?', and just posing that question already pre-supposes that a link is possible and even likely.

So in this chapter, I am exploring how language impacts on us and others, the habits of language that may be giving us an impact we hadn't intended and how we might address these habits going forward.

HOW DOES LANGUAGE IMPACT ON US AND THE PEOPLE WE COMMUNICATE WITH?

In Chapter 2, I introduced the NLP Communication Model and the idea that our brain (unconsciously) filters the information coming in. Two of these filters are language and memories. So how we hear and interpret the words coming into us is affected by what these words have come to mean to us and what associations they have. An example of this is the word *smoke*. When I have asked people what came to mind on hearing this word, there are a range of reactions: from the homely smell and warm associations of autumn leaves burning in the garden from one to another who experienced a house fire in their home which elicited frightening memories.

Similarly, when I hear people use the word *manipulation* when referring to handling conversations skilfully with other people, I feel the need to check out how they hear that word: as to me it implies someone being underhand and disrespectful. More often than not it turns out that their associations with the word are far more innocent than mine!

These same filters also govern the language we use to others and usually give some clues as to how we are thinking and what we believe. (I will expand on this in the next section of this chapter.)

At the same time, we can't know for sure how the language we use impacts another person and that's when we need to pay attention to the feedback we are getting, verbally or non-verbally.

The language we use is once again in effect 'shaping' our brain. The experience-dependent neuroplasticity referred to in the previous chapter, means what we say about and to ourselves habitually, is over time forming neural networks which could either be supporting strengths or weaknesses!

As set out in Chapter 7 our unconscious mind has the characteristics of a 5 year old child, eager to please and wanting clear direction. It takes what we say literally and looks to prove us right: whether we are criticising or praising ourselves, it filters for the evidence to prove us right. It lacks a sense of humour and so when we say something we regard as modest and self –deprecating like: "Oh I am rubbish at that", it treats it as a fact. So for managing our impact on self and others we really need to mind our language!

WHAT IS THE STRUCTURE OF WHAT WE SAY TELLING US AND OTHERS?

Language has a Surface Structure and a Deeper Structure:

Surface Structure: Conscious mind expressing a thought which is only a shorthand version of the original.

Deeper Structure: Unconscious Mind 'filters' the original thought by deleting distorting and generalising (As referred to in the NLP Communication Model in Chapter 2)

An example of this might be someone saying: "My boss doesn't rate me". When we hear this we might be tempted to sympathise or offer advice, in effect, taking what is said at face value and interpreting it through our own 'map of the world'.

On the other hand, we might ask some questions instead, and rather than interpret, start to explore what is behind that statement. This is not just for our clarity, but with the direct intention to help the speaker re-examine their own thinking. Even if we simply ask 'How do you know that?' the person is prompted to think how they came to that conclusion and may find scant evidence to back up the statement. It may have been driven by negative beliefs about themselves or their boss and our question may prompt them to reappraise what they have said, and modify their view. As the filtering has been done unconsciously the person will not necessarily be aware of the process (the deletions, distortions and generalisations that led to that statement).

Our everyday speech is littered with these patterns, which in NLP are collectively referred to as 'Meta-Model' (originally created by Richard Bandler and John Grinder). They are so commonplace it is easy to let them slip by our notice and leave them unchallenged. Here is a summary of the patterns and the questions you might ask someone else, (or indeed yourself) to 'recover' information that has been 'lost' as your brain has filtered your thoughts:

"She thinks she is being clever" – this is an example of a *Mind Read*, where the speaker presumes to know what someone else is thinking and indeed he/she may well be convinced they are right and their actions will reflect this belief. A possible question to get them thinking differently is:

"How do you know that?"

"It's stupid to approach it in that way!" – this is where someone expresses their opinion as a fact (aka a *Lost Performative* for anyone wanting the Meta Model title!). This way of speaking might get someone else's back up, and /or the person saying it can be reinforcing their own beliefs with a statement like this. A possible question to get them thinking differently is:

"In whose opinion is it stupid?"
or
"By what standard do you judge ...?"

"Meetings bore me!" – this is an example of *Cause > Effect* (referred to in earlier chapters), where the speaker is putting themselves at Effect and therefore taking no responsibility for the situation, or getting out of it. A possible question to get them thinking differently is:

"How do meetings cause you to be bored?"

"She hasn't invited me to the meeting so she doesn't think I have anything to contribute" – this is a *Complex Equivalence*, where someone puts some facts together and reaches a conclusion that may be a step too far. It may be true of course, but it is an assumption that they are making without checking it out. A possible question to get them thinking differently is:

"How does not inviting you mean she thinks you have nothing to contribute?"

"I either apply for this promotion or leave" – this statement is a *Pre-supposition* (of the un-resourceful kind!) i.e. it presupposes something unhelpful, in this case, that there are only 2 choices. A possible question to open up more choices is:

"Who says there are only two options?"

"I never say the right thing" – this is an example of a *Universal Quantifier* and is usually an exaggeration. Other examples are all, every, no one, everyone. Using this language, particularly in a business environment, can make what might be basically a good point seem ill-thought out, and therefore easily dismissed. A possible question to get them thinking differently is:

"Never?"

or

"Has there ever been a time when you have?"

"We shouldn't negotiate on this" or *"I can't do that"* – these are examples of *Modal Operators of Necessity and Possibility*, or in simpler terms limiting rules and assumptions that we might impose on ourselves or others. They can keep us on a narrow thinking track or stop us from even attempting to do something differently. Possible questions to generate some new thinking are:

"What would happen if we/you did?"

or

"What stops you?"

"My education was poor" – this use of the word Education is called a *Nominalization*. It is usually a verb that has been turned

into a noun you physically cannot see and has a range of possible meanings – I often refer to these as 'fat' words (these can be thought of as nouns that cannot be put in a wheelbarrow, unlike a table for instance). Other examples of nominalizations could be 'Success', 'Knowhow' or 'Communication'. The danger is that the listener may make their own assumption about what is meant and then agree! A way to recover what the person actually means is by turning it back into a verb or asking questions to understand the meaning:

"How were you educated?"

or

"What was it about how you were educated that was poor?"

"I told him to man up!" – this is an *Unspecified Verb* in that the speaker has not specified how the person is meant to do that. I was given this example in a conversation with an HR Director… it is unclear if she noticed my eyes widening at her comment! I recovered her meaning by asking:

"How specifically did you want him to do that?"

"I am concerned" – this is a statement left hanging for the listener to potentially put their own meaning to it, called a *Simple Deletion*. For clarity you can ask:

"About what ...?"

"Some people are never happy" – in this case, it isn't clear to whom the speaker is referring and can also be an exaggeration (called an *Unspecified Referential Index*). So to check this out and avoid ambiguity you can ask:

"Who do you mean by some people?"

"I want them to do more" – this is another example of a real client conversation I have had called a *Comparative Deletion*. The challenge was to find out what his team were doing now and what 'more' would look like. Not easy questions to consider and yet without these answers, we would not know if we had succeeded. So I started to recover his meaning by asking:

"Compared to what...?"
and
"What do you mean by more?"

The correct titles of these patterns may not be important to you, nonetheless starting to notice these patterns in everyday speech, opens up a way to help ourselves or other people rethink some limiting patterns of thinking or assumptions. When we use language like this unchallenged, we are not only expressing our limiting patterns of thinking, we may be reinforcing them. These are barriers to our success and happiness that we are putting in our own path.

The examples given have potentially negative effects for the person saying them or others around them. We may hear these patterns in far more innocuous contexts too, and in those situations it may be more damaging to the relationship to challenge them, not to mention pointless to do so. E.g. If someone says "She is lovely" it would churlish to come back with "Who says?"

Even when someone is saying something with a negative implication for them, helping them explore, and maintain a good rapport, will require a respectful, adult voice tone avoiding interrogation. Our intention to help is the guiding principle here. Asking too many questions about a statement someone has just made, could easily move from prompting a rethink, to causing an argument. As ever a good place to start is with noticing...and challenging our own thinking!

WEASEL WORDS?

A course delegate of mine christened the following words as 'Weasel' words. This usually means words or statements that are intentionally ambiguous or misleading, and yet the words listed below are potentially more misleading still, because we may use them innocently in our everyday speech. It is only when we listen again we may find what we are actually saying might lead the listener to take another meaning entirely:

But or However:

I really like how you approached that report **but** I think you could have made the conclusion clearer.

The BUT wipes out the first part of the sentence.

Alternative: I really like how you approached that report **and** think you could have made the conclusion clearer.

Try:

I will **try** to write the report.

The TRY creates uncertainty in the mind of the speaker and the listener.

Alternative: I will write the report.

Should:

I think you **should** handle the meeting this way.

The SHOULD sounds parental and implies one way of doing something.

Alternative: I think you **could** handle the meeting this way.

If:

If you are able to use your learning from this book.

In this context IF implies doubt, when certainty would be more useful.

Alternative: **When** you are able to use your learning from this book.

Difficult:

Handling this situation will be **difficult**.

The use of the word DIFFICULT can signal a block as many people hear this word as interchangeable with impossible.

Alternative: Handling this situation will be a **challenge**.

I can't:

I can't get this to you by Monday morning.

Whilst this may be a true statement many people hear 'I CAN'T' as 'I won't' and can engender an aggressive reply (as people working in call centres can attest!)

Alternative: **I can** get it to you by Monday afternoon.

Unfortunately:

Unfortunately, that is not our policy.

The use of UNFORTUNATELY particularly at the beginning of a sentence may stop the other person from listening to or reading what comes next. Nor does it add anything, except perhaps in the example given could suggest company policy is wrong.

Alternative: That is not our policy.

SELF TALKING OURSELVES TO SUCCESS: LESSONS FROM MUHAMMED ALI?

"The meaning of a communication is the message that is understood"

In Chapter 4, I introduced the pre-suppositions of NLP and this is another. It is not what we intended to say that matters, it is how the listener receives it… really useful to remember when we are considering our impact. Although it is not just other people our language has an impact on, it is also ourselves.

I have referred to the unconscious mind in previous Chapters and that it hears what we say about and to ourselves and looks to prove us right. So what is the message that our unconscious mind is getting and what do we want that to be?

Muhammed Ali, considered to be the world's greatest heavyweight boxer, was also someone who knew the impact that words could have on himself and others, particularly his opponents in the ring.

He famously said to George Foreman in the later stages of their famous 'Rumble in the Jungle':

"Is that all you've got, George?"

Now that must have been pretty dispiriting for Foreman to hear and at a time when he was struggling anyway. For himself though, he also knew the importance of his self-talk:

"It's the repetition of affirmations that leads to belief. And once that belief becomes a deep conviction, things begin to happen."

His most famous affirmation was of course:

"I am the greatest"

This is a brilliant example of a positive affirmation because he put it in the present tense: he was saying it before he was 'the greatest', whilst he was the greatest and indeed to the end of his days. We can use this same structure to create our own positive affirmations to make things happen for ourselves:

1. Consider what you want to create in your life e.g. success in an interview or a great working relationship with your colleagues

2. Phrase it in the present tense – everything is created in your mind before becoming reality – state it as if it is true NOW.

3. Phrase it in terms of what you DO want rather than what you don't.

4. Make it short and easily remembered.

Choose or create affirmations that are powerful for you, and with them nurture the belief that they can be true. People often feel a little resistance to some affirmations, so just notice this if it happens and recognize you are creating new neural networks to help you create more of the life, (and relationships) that you want.

Another useful technique Ali used alongside his language was a visualisation technique he called creating his 'Future History'. As preparation Ali imagined the fight in detail up to the point of being declared the champion at the end, his arms raised and the crowd cheering. He repeated this numerous times pre-fight, so when he entered the ring he was mentally and physically at his peak, and he had already won the fight in his mind. He declared:

"The man who has no imagination has no wings."

As referred to in Chapter 4 under the NLP pre-supposition:

Memory and imagination are
wired on the same circuits.

This visualisation technique is one used by sportsmen and women today... and anyone that wants to 'programme' themselves for success. Here's how you can create your own 'Future History':

1. Consider/think about a goal or outcome that you would like to achieve

2. Visualise achieving it and notice what you are hearing, seeing and feeling as you do

3. Repeat steps 1 and 2 as many times as you like... and as you do ramp it up by making the colour and the brightness of the picture just right…and the volume and qualities of the sounds and the feelings just as you want them.

Creating your Future History is a skill like any other… so it really benefits from practice and repetition!

Exercise:

As you finish this chapter on language and consider the changes you might want to make, here are some ideas:

1. Think about how you would speak to someone you love and care about. How would you speak to them before an important event, or at a time when they might need encouragement? And consider how it would be if you spoke to yourself in this way too...

2. Create a positive affirmation (using the structure in the last section) for your next working day/tomorrow/ an important event where you want to do well. Make it punchy and memorable and then say it to yourself at the start of and throughout the day/event.

3. Add to your positive affirmation with the visualisation technique set out in the previous section.

4. Practice 'noticing' the Meta-model patterns set out in this chapter when you are in a meeting and at a point where you are not directly involved in the conversation. Pick 2-3 patterns to look out for in each meeting.

KEY POINTS:

» What we say and how we say it has a greater impact on ourselves and others than we might think – the language we use over time 'shapes' our brain

» Language has a Surface Structure which is the conscious mind's shorthand for our thinking at our Deeper level

» The Deeper Structure of our language is where the unconscious 'filters' our thinking by deleting, distorting and generalising

» Surface structure language gives clues to how we are thinking at a Deeper level – in NLP the unhelpful patterns that can be observed are termed Meta Model

» Meta Model patterns of speech indicate the flawed thinking that is getting in the way of our success and happiness

» When we spot these patterns we can ask ourselves or others questions to recover the 'lost' information and achieve more balanced thinking

Chapter 7
Ooops...Who's Driving?

HOW DO I GET TO 'AYE AYE CAPTAIN!'

I have been delighted on a few occasions now when course delegates are introducing themselves and saying what they do, when a delegate has said: "I drive a ship for a living". The reaction from the others has been little short of amazement, as to most landlubbers (like me) the idea of driving a ship is so far from our experience. There is awe at the idea of managing a crew with a wide variety of skills, the technical knowledge required, as well as knowledge of the sea. Surely a captain can't know everything?

What emerges is the trust the captain has to have in the crew, the challenge of keeping skills up to date and of generally introducing and sustaining change to a large busy crew, many of whom the captain may not know well.

The relationship between the conscious and the unconscious has been likened to a captain of a ship and the crew. The captain may be in charge but it is the crew that really makes things happen – without the crew's cooperation the ship will not go the way the captain wants, or at all. If what the captain asks is new, different or out of the ordinary, the crew need time to learn and adjust. It is also true that the crew need leadership, without clear direction from the captain the ship will be rudderless.

So our conscious mind has the illusion of control in one sense and yet when it works mindfully and cooperatively with the unconscious on the other, it can move our 'ship' in the direction we want it to go.

HOW SIGNIFICANT IS THE UNCONSCIOUS MIND IN DETERMINING OUR BEHAVIOUR?

In the foregoing Chapters and in Chapter 2 specifically, I referred to the unconscious mind and its dominance in determining our behaviour. The concept of the unconscious was popularized by the Austrian neurologist and psychoanalyst Sigmund Freud and it was his assertion that as only 10% of our brain activity was conscious, so 90% was unconscious and the key driver of our behaviour. More recent studies have indicated that the unconscious part could be higher even than that:

"An enormous portion of cognitive activity is non-conscious. Figuratively speaking, it could be 99 percent; we probably will never know precisely how much is outside awareness."

Emmanuel Donchin, director of the Laboratory for Cognitive Psychophysiology at the University of Illinois

UNCONSCIOUS OR SUBCONSCIOUS MIND?

Before I go on to discuss the unconscious further, let me clarify the words I am using. The terms unconscious and subconscious are often referred to interchangeably. In fact, the term *subconscious* was coined by psychologist Pierre Janet and refers to information that we are not actively aware of in that moment in time: an example might be the little toe on your left foot, which you may not be consciously aware of until you read this sentence i.e. it is readily brought into your consciousness. So as the prefix *'sub'* suggests, it is below our consciousness and easily accessed, whilst the prefix *'un'* in *unconscious* indicates a lack of awareness and so harder to access. Both subconscious and unconscious are contained in the 90% referred to in the previous section, as this is everything that is 'off-line' and not in our conscious awareness in that moment.

I will use the terms conscious and unconscious minds only.

WHAT DO WE KNOW ABOUT THE UNCONSCIOUS?

In the development of NLP Richard Bandler and John Grinder were influenced by, amongst other things, developments in neuroscience, which have been considerable in the last 50 years. Many theories have emerged and some are difficult to prove. What we do know is that the unconscious is powerful and research into it is ongoing. Nonetheless, we can verify much of what is understood about the unconscious from our own everyday life observations.

How the unconscious is viewed has changed over time moving from seeing the conscious/unconscious in terms of good and bad, to the modern view that there are mental processes that we are aware of (conscious), and others that we are unaware of (unconscious).

As set out in Chapter 2 it is generally accepted that the unconscious is like a 5 year old child simple, innocent, eager to please, wanting clear instruction and likely to take what is said to it literally. Additionally, in his book "Integrate The Shadow, Master Your Path" Dr Matthew James starts by summarising some of the key characteristics and duties of the unconscious that we are aware of:

- It runs the body and protects the body
- Organises memories
- Aims to give you what it thinks you need
- It is highly moral (i.e. the moral code you have been raised with that is)
- It will go for the easiest route to get what you say you want

- Takes what you say personally
- It is quick to make associations between new information and existing knowledge so helping us to learn.

The unconscious is working constantly and we cannot turn it off, which is just as well as it is controlling the functioning of our bodies whether we are awake or asleep. We do not consciously make our heart beat or digest food for example. Its primary function is to preserve our lives and keep us in good health, so if you step into the street in front of a bus, initially you jump back out of the way without processing the situation in the conscious mind. In effect, the 'thinking' part of the brain is bypassed and the flight/fight response kicks in.

In everyday life, this vital trait can give us a problem. The unconscious cannot easily distinguish between a physical, emotional or verbal threat. In a situation where we are physically threatened, our physical response of fighting or running away serves to dissipate the stress hormones. When the 'threat' is verbal or emotional (probably more common in everyday life!) the stress hormones are not dissipated, exaggerating the tension and stress, and even sometimes causing us to say something we later regret.

HOW CAN KNOWING ALL THIS ABOUT OUR UNCONSCIOUS HELP US?

So for the good of our health, achieving our goals and our impact on others our conscious mind needs to work effectively with our unconscious as John Bargh observes. When we do this consistently we can build new habits of behaviour.

> *"We are what we repeatedly do. Excellence, then, is not an act, but a habit"*
> *Aristotle*

- *Managing our 'threat' response:* instead of challenging conversations being treated as a threat we can start to 'reframe' our thinking. Embracing the pre-suppositions of NLP set out in Chapter 4 can help us here – when we see someone else's behaviour differently or view ourselves differently, the fear, anxiety or threat is reduced and the 'thinking' part of our brain can stay in control. This way of thinking needs practice and with repetition, over time we can form new habits of response.

- *Recognising our 'map' of the world is unique:* In Chapter 3 I referred to the work of Wilder Penfield who demonstrated how all our life experiences are recorded and stored. Obviously, we have a great deal recorded that we cannot easily access and yet it is shaping our thoughts and our reactions – in effect, this is our map of the world and worth remembering it is likely to be very different from others. Our reactions to them will be shaped by our map. Also in Chapter 4 looking at the pre-supposition 'Structures we see in others mirrors structures in ourselves' I said 'everyone we meet is a mirror'. Their map might be different from ours and yet the things we notice about their behaviour may be telling us something about ourselves and what we may need to address.

- **Setting goals:** Taking into account the 'childlike' nature of the unconscious and the fact that it takes things literally, is very significant when we look at how we speak about and to ourselves, it has no sense of humour! Just saying "I want to be successful" is too vague; something like "I want to be managing this department or equivalent in two years" is more likely to programme ourselves for the success we want. Dr Matthew James also points out that the unconscious works on the principle of the least effort… so a tiny pay increase may signal success and job done, not what the conscious had in mind at all.

- **Speaking about ourselves:** In Chapter 6, I referred to the fact that we sometimes make statements in a humorous way which might actually be having the opposite effect to the one intended. For example, we might say in a self-deprecating way "Oh I'm a disaster at presentations!". Our intention may be to appear modest but our unconscious will interpret that literally and then helpfully seek out the information to prove us right. (Fortunately as said earlier, our unconscious responds well to repetition to build habits and learning, so reading this point a few times should be all to the good!)

- **Being clear about what we want:** Often we confuse our unconscious by saying what we want in terms of what we don't want – possibly the result of many sentences from our parents starting with the word "Don't..." As Martin Shervington points out in his humorously titled book "Don't Think About Purple Spotted Oranges!", the unconscious cannot process a negative, so cannot easily distinguish between what you do and do not want it to do. If I say "Don't worry", your brain needs to create the idea of worry before it can get rid of it and the image or idea is already there. So if we say things like "I don't want to get nervous in this meeting", notice what the unconscious hears... and what would work better?

- **Speaking about and to other people:** Another trait of the unconscious Matthew James points out which is perhaps not so obvious, is that it takes things personally. I have referred on a few occasions now to the idea that 'everyone we meet is a mirror', based on the work of Carl Jung. What this means practically is that how we speak to or view others is taken by our unconscious to refer to us. We may have heard someone describe another and thought 'pot and kettle situation here' i.e. they could be speaking about themselves. I have been working with a lady that is very sharply critical of her boss and colleagues... and unsurprisingly that critical approach is reflected in how she speaks about herself, which in turn is having a detrimental effect on her own self-esteem. Happily, the reverse is also true, often people who are confident in their own abilities inspire others to be the best they can be too.

"If you treat an individual as he is, he will remain as he is. But if you treat him as if he were what he ought to be and could be, he will become what he ought and could be."

Johann Wolfgang von Goethe, German writer and statesman

The fortunate thing is that the brain's ability to learn and form new neural pathways means that when we take into consideration how the unconscious works, the conscious mind can work with the unconscious over a period of time to learn new things, form new habits and get different results.

HOW DOES THIS RELATE TO THE 'DRIVERS' IN TRANSACTIONAL ANALYSIS?

In Chapter 3 I outlined the theory of Transactional Analysis to explain the reactions and interactions between people. If you are familiar with Transactional Analysis you will know that body of work also refers to 'Drivers' of behaviour. So I think it is also useful to look at these 'drivers' to help in our understanding of our own and others behaviour; as well as highlighting perhaps where some new thinking and new habits would be valuable.

In 1975 Taibi Kahler identified 5 'Drivers' which can be at the root of dysfunctional behaviour. Whilst this is a separate body of work from NLP, how these 'drivers' have been created and become embedded becomes obvious when you consider the characteristics of the unconscious mind discussed in this chapter. They can also be evidenced in the Meta-Model language referred to in Chapter 6. Their origins are in the 'messages' we receive in early life which form our values, beliefs, habits and even our moral code. As these have become embedded in our unconscious we may not notice them and therefore do not challenge them, even though they may be causing difficulties for ourselves and in our relationships with others.

The five 'drivers' Kahler identified are:

- **Be Perfect** – in the grip of this driver, everything has to be just so and 'Be Perfects' will spend time and worry about achieving the standards that they hold in their heads: standards that are not necessarily required by others around them. They may achieve great things with high-quality output but may hold these expectations of others too and find critical feedback hard to take… although they may be the ones to dish it out to others who do not meet their standards.

- **Be Strong** – people with this driver feel they cannot show any vulnerability or ask for help. They expect themselves and others to be strong and whilst they will help others before themselves, they can also show contempt for those they regard as weak. They are good in a crisis and will get things done but bottled up emotions can explode or be turned inwards. If the person is managing others they may even be reluctant to delegate.

- **Hurry Up** – this person will be energetic and enthusiastic juggling a number of things at a time. When given work they will deliver it quickly but can easily take on too much and then complain about it. They will also put themselves and others under time pressure by underestimating the time needed to complete a task.

- **Please Others** – a person with this driver will put the needs, wants and desires of others over their own. They seek to please, seek approval of others, worry about how they will be perceived and find it hard to say no. Whilst they are good company and work well in a team, in extreme cases, they can find positions of authority a challenge.

- **Try Hard** – people in the grip of this driver talk more about the effort they have put in than the achievement – it is not ok to succeed easily – indeed they will use the 'try' word a lot. They will do their utmost in situations, be persistent and will help others in these circumstances. They might want praise but find it difficult to accept and over a period of time this behaviour leads to burn out.

Maybe you recognised yourself in some of these descriptions – if not, look again, as when I have used a questionnaire to identify these with individuals previously, I have never had a zero score emerge. In other words, there is a little, and sometimes a lot, of these in all of us. They can be 'invisible' to us to start with, because when we are in the grip of these 'drivers', in our map of the world we are doing a 'good' thing, and in times of stress we exhibit these behaviours even more.

At some level, these are 'good' things to do and yet very quickly overuse of them can have a negative impact on ourselves, our work and others around us. How confusing then is it for us to be doing a 'good' thing for the 'right' reasons and find other people frustrated and critical of us? In these cases, the gap between our intention and our impact is potentially a yawning one.

> *"You cannot stop the waves, but*
> *you can learn to surf"*
> John Kabbat-Zinn Professor of Medicine Emeritus
> and the creator of the Stress Reduction Clinic, Health
> Care and Centre for Mindfulness in Medicine

WHAT HAPPENS WHEN THE CAPTAIN WORKS WITH THE CREW?

So when our 'captain' i.e. our conscious mind understands the 'crew' our unconscious mind, they can work more effectively together to:

- Manage our behaviour and responses to challenging people and situations
- Reduce stress and anxiety levels
- Programme ourselves and others more effectively for success
- Give effective, constructive feedback to ourselves and others
- Create new resourceful habits of behaviour

All of which can really shift the impact that we have on ourselves and others.

And the good news is our brain is capable of change. At one time it was thought that neuroplasticity only occurred during certain periods in childhood. While it's certainly true plastic change happens much more easily when we are young, your brain's capability to make changes can last a lifetime.

> *"There's a traditional saying that the mind takes the shape it rests upon; the modern update is that the brain takes the shape the mind rests upon."*
>
> Rick Hanson, PhD and Psychologist from "Just One Thing: Developing a Buddha Brain One Simple Practice at a Time"

Rick Hanson's point is of course if your focus is worry, your brain will develop those neural structures, if your focus is your self-worth your brain will take the shape of that too.

Exercise:

In Chapter 6 I suggested some exercises around noticing language patterns that might be limiting success, happiness or opportunity. Also creating positive affirmations for yourself and a compelling vision for what you want.

1. If you haven't done these exercises yet, their importance may be clearer to you now, so this may be a good time to do them.

2. If you have completed the exercises at the end of Chapter 6, take some time now to reflect on what has changed already as a result of shifting your language and/or your thinking.

3. Consider Kahler's 'Drivers' and how they apply to you. Perhaps ask a colleague if they observe any of these in you. Take your most noticeable driver and consider... what do I need to ask myself to start to shift my thinking here? For example: If your driver is 'Be Perfect' you could ask yourself 'What is actually required of me?' and /or 'How is this driver impacting on my friends, family or work colleagues?' 'What is my first step in doing something about it?

KEY POINTS:

» The Conscious and Unconscious minds are like the Captain and Crew of a ship – they need to work together to go in the right direction

» The Unconscious refers to the part that is 'off-line' at any one time and it accounts for 90% + of our behaviour – the real driver

» The unconscious is like a 5 year old child – simple, innocent, eager to please, wanting clear instruction and likely to take what is said to it literally

» Key characteristics or duties of the Unconscious Mind are:
   » Managing Memories and Emotions
   » Running and Preserving the Body
   » Interpreting the Outside World and Ourselves
   » Helping Us To Learn

» The brain is capable of change – neuroplasticity lasts a lifetime

» In Transactional Analysis there are 5 key 'Drivers' of our behaviour: Be Perfect, Please Others, Be Strong, Hurry Up, Try Hard. We develop these in early childhood and these are up for change if we recognise them and want to do something about the dysfunctional behaviour they create.

Chapter 8
What Just Happened There... Helping Myself?

Walk a Mile in His Moccasins by Mary T. Lathrap

Just walk a mile in his moccasins
Before you abuse, criticize and accuse.
If just for one hour, you could find a way
To see through his eyes, instead of your own muse.

Brother, there but for the grace of God go you and I.
Just for a moment, slip into his mind and traditions
And see the world through his spirit and eyes
Before you cast a stone or falsely judge his conditions.

I have just taken an excerpt from Mary Lathrap's poem and found it is hard to know what to leave out, as it is well worth reading in full. This poem is credited with being the original source of the Native American aphorism *"Before you judge a man, walk a mile in his shoes (moccasins)"*. Whether you read one or all ten verses, the message is the same: show empathy, don't judge others too harshly, we cannot know what it is like in their map of the world. In return, others are likely to respond to us more positively.

At the start of this book, I used the metaphor of being inside a house and not really knowing how we are being perceived from the outside – this is, in fact, the essence of the 'Intention Impact Conundrum'. We have looked at addressing this by getting feedback from others, but how can we get some perspective for ourselves: time to reflect and experience what it is to be on the receiving end of us? What impact could such insights have on us? What could we learn about how it is for others that could really shift our thinking and behaviour?

WHAT GETS IN THE WAY OF SEEING MY OWN BEHAVIOUR?

> *"Learning is experience. Everything else is just information."*
> Albert Einstein

When I drive away from a meeting or a conversation, particularly if I have been unhappy about it in some way, I frustratingly go back over what was said by whom. I often think 'this is what I should have said', which apparently the French call 'l'esprit d'escalier' or 'staircase wit', way too late for the clever riposte, and only another source of frustration. The problem with this internal conversation and my 'too late' pithy reply, is that is conducted entirely from my point of view, and I do not consider how it was for the other person/people in the interaction. Hence my learning from this replayed conversation is limited. I know I am not alone in this.

I was working with a group of shift managers from a manufacturing business when one of them whom I will call John, told a story about being involved in a physical fight with a colleague, whom I will call Peter. He was angry about it and could not see how else he could have handled the situation, much less that the other person had any justification for his behaviour.

So without preamble, I asked John to sit as he was sitting when the conversation with his colleague started, and to look across at where his colleague was seated. Immediately the conversation and the emotions came back, and he was there in the moment. I then asked him to stand up, made some jokes with his other colleagues, (to break his 'state'[1]), who were watching with some amusement and asked him then to take up Peter's sitting position, which was on the other side of the room from where John was sitting. From there I got him to re-run the conversation from this viewpoint. Almost immediately he looked at me in surprise and exclaimed: "I would have hit me if I had been Peter!". We all laughed, as it was apparent he had had a real insight in that short time. I then asked him to take up the position of a 'fly on the wall' and look at the conversation from a more neutral viewpoint. From there he was able to see the encounter more dispassionately and as a result give John (himself) some advice. When we finished the exercise, he was in a very different state and much more willing to take responsibility for his own actions.

The post script to that story is that he phoned me a few months later to wish me a happy Christmas and thank me for the course, to which he added "...and I haven't hit anybody since!" even then he was still reflecting on the exercise!!

What I did, (without explaining to John at the time) was to take him through an NLP exercise called Perceptual Positions, which I know you may well be familiar with. From my experience, this is one of the most often used NLP exercise, mainly because of the learning it yields, whether someone else takes you through it, or you do it by yourself.

The exercise was developed by John Grinder (Co-founder of NLP) and Judith De Lozier (involved in the development of NLP since the 1970s), who modelled therapists like Milton Erikson and Virginia Satir. They found that quite independently these therapists were using similar techniques of getting their clients to take up different physical positions to gain more insight into how a situation might be for another person. What this is not, is a 'mind read', we cannot claim to know what another person is thinking, but by taking up someone else's physical posture and moving out of our own space we can get some useful insights as to how it is for them.

When my Dad died many years ago now, a few months later my
Mother and I went to the Donegal coast in the north-west of
Ireland for a weekend break. While there we went walking on the
beach and our conversation was stilted as if there was little common
understanding. I felt this very strongly and started paying attention
to what I was doing and what she was doing. I was looking up at
the blue sky and out to sea, while she was walking, hands in pockets
looking down at the sand. When I took up her walking posture and
eye-line, the conversation started to change and changed dramatically: in effect, I stepped into her map of the world and met her
there. When we got to the end of the beach, we sat down on the
rocks and really talked in a way we hadn't before. It turned out I
didn't have to 'walk a mile' to experience more about what it was
like in my mother's shoes, but stepping out of my own was a big part
of the process.

TAKING 'PERCEPTUAL POSITIONS' TO UNDERSTAND AND SHIFT YOUR IMPACT

"Thinking and learning are not all in our head.
On the contrary, the body plays an integral
part in all our intellectual processes from our
earliest moments right through to old age."
Dr Carla Hannaford, neurophysiologist and educator from
"Smart Moves: Why Learning Is Not All in Your Head"

So Perceptual Positions is an exercise that uses movement to facilitate the learning and new thinking. The basic steps in this exercise are:

- Position 1 – my viewpoint
- Position 2 – the other person's viewpoint
- Position 3 – the observer viewpoint, the 'fly on the wall'

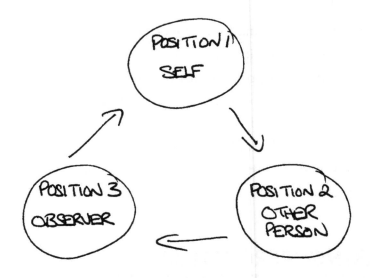

You can successfully take yourself through this exercise or get someone else to guide you. Whichever option you choose, it is important to do it kinaesthetically (physically moving around) because of the strong link between learning and moving, and because this process also uses a technique called spatial anchoring, i.e. when a specific space becomes anchored in our unconscious as having a special meaning or association.

This process can be used to:

- Get some insight on how you are impacting on another person or group.
- Revisit a conversation or situation where you were not happy with the outcome and want to generate some ideas about what you could do or say differently, to improve the outcome.
- Plan how you could handle a future interaction with another individual or a group to make the impact you want.

If you are using this approach for the first time, it is useful to use a mildly unsatisfactory situation. This will enable you to become familiar with the process avoiding too much emotional content. What may surprise you is the level of learning even in these situations.

So to start, choose a situation/conversation about which you would value more information and follow these steps – for simplicity in describing the process I am assuming a face to face conversation between you and another person:

1. Decide on where positions 1 and 2 will be. If the communication was seated place two chairs at the same distance and aspect as they were in the original conversation.

2. **Position 1: YOU:** take up this first position seated or standing as appropriate. In your mind take yourself back into the location where this conversation took place, sit or stand as you were, and bring it into the present. Notice the layout and what you are seeing hearing and feeling before the conversation started.

Look across at the other person in the interaction and notice how they are sitting/standing and the look on their face before the conversation starts. Then run the conversation like a video in your head, noticing your feelings and any physical changes as it progresses.

Break your state[1] by moving out of this position, and then turning around or taking your thoughts to another subject for a moment. Then move into Position 2.

3. **Position 2: OTHER PERSON:** in this position take up the seating/ standing position of the other person as the conversation started. Look across at Position 1 noticing the posture and facial expression and how this looks from here. Notice the feelings engendered as you do so. Notice what you are seeing differently already. Then run the conversation like a video in your head, noticing your feelings from this position and any physical changes as it progresses.

Break your state by moving out of this position, and then turning around or taking your thoughts to another subject for a moment. Then take up Position 3, choose a place where you can see both parties easily and far enough away to be able to take a dispassionate view of the scene.

4. **Position 3: OBSERVER:** from this position observe both people in the interaction, their posture and how they are regarding one another. Then run the conversation like a video, noticing what is different from this viewpoint. While from

here you may see things that both parties could have done differently, the only one whom you can directly influence is yourself in Position 1. (NB this is also putting you at 'Cause' as referred to in Chapter 1.)

So from this position consider what advice you would give yourself to improve this interaction (it might be your physical position, it might be what you could say or how you say it or even who opens the conversation.) Give that advice to yourself in Position 1 and check if it is accepted. (If there is resistance or it seems difficult to see how you could have changed this situation, consider what one little thing could have improved the situation just a tiny bit.)

Then ask 'Is there any higher learning in this for me?' i.e. is what happened here evidence of a pattern of behaviour that you have exhibited in other circumstances that is not serving you or your relationships with others? Then give that advice to yourself in Position 1 and check if it is accepted.

Break your state by moving out of this position, and then turning around or taking your thoughts to another subject for a moment. Then go back into Position 1.

5. **Position 1: YOU:** this time take the advice of your Observer and re-run the situation, noticing what difference making these changes creates in yourself and the other person. You can end the exercise here or stand up, break state and go back into Position 2 to experience the changes from that viewpoint.

You can also go round all the positions again if you want to make further changes.

The basic Perceptual Positions exercise set out above can be very revealing and allows us to get more information about someone else's map of the world. You also may notice the link to Muhammed Ali's visualisation technique described in Chapter 6 and the pre-supposition:

Memory and imagination are wired on the same circuits

This exercise is not simply about generating ideas about what you could have done; it is about programming yourself to handle similar interactions differently in the future, blurring the lines in effect between what you have imagined vividly and your memories. In Chapter 7, I referred to the unconscious mind and specifically how it responds to clear instructions. This exercise gives the unconscious a clear instruction about what will work better.

I work with an organisation that has a call centre, and I had the group reflecting on difficult conversations with customers using this exercise. They all reported that they found the exercise useful, whilst also saying they wished that they had handled it better at the time (l'esprit d'escalier again!). A few months later I visited the call centre, and one of the team was keen to tell me about something that had happened earlier that week. She had been on a 'tricky' call and when she disconnected, one of her colleagues rolled back her chair and gave her feedback, there and then, about how well she had handled the call. It was then she said she realised it was 'just like the exercise we had done on the course!' She hadn't remembered the exercise at the time she was speaking to the customer; she just handled the situation differently and only retrospectively saw the link with the exercise.

WHAT ELSE CAN I DO TO UNDERSTAND AND IMPROVE MY IMPACT?

This exercise can have quite long-lasting effects on how you impact on others and is a way of working on your impact that you can do alone. Also, you can add other elements to it to help you achieve the outcomes you want and /or expand your field of resources:

Some other useful questions: when in the Observer position you may notice that your motivation to solve the issue or to take responsibility for solving it is doubtful, (being willing to be 'at Cause' is not always a given). In these situations some useful questions to ask yourself are:

- What will happen when I solve this problem?
- What won't happen when I solve this problem?
- What will happen if I don't solve this problem?
- What won't happen if I don't solve this problem? (This question will expose any secondary gain i.e. benefits of doing nothing which could be undermining your resolve.)

Other people present: often in an interaction, there may have been other people present, and it may be quite revealing to step into 'their shoes' and see it from their viewpoint. This could be useful in looking at the original conversation, or to do an 'ecology check'[2] on the ideas proposed by your Observer – it is possible after all to improve your impact on one person and unintentionally damage your relationship with another!

Other resourceful positions: another way of generating ideas, developed by Stephen Gilligan and Robert Dilts in their Generative Coaching work is to 'step into the shoes' of another person who could be a resource to you, regardless of whether they were present at the original conversation or not. It could be someone alive or dead, someone known to you personally or simply someone whom you have admired from a distance. This position could also be a useful 'ecology' checker as well.

WHAT ABOUT USING THIS EXERCISE TO PLAN A MEETING?

When I set up my business, one of the first meetings I had was with a client who I had met and knew a little about. We were meeting to discuss using psychometric testing in his business's recruitment process. I wanted to ensure that I handled the meeting effectively and that my impact on him was a positive one.

Having never visited his office I knew nothing of the layout, but I knew we would most likely be seated for the meeting. So I set out the chairs in my office, and went through how I would open the meeting (i.e. Position 1). I then moved into his seat (Position 2) and experienced the opening from his viewpoint, the result was dramatic: I felt overwhelmed by this woman's energy and the amount of information she was giving me! Moving into my Observer position the advice was clear: sit back, slow down and let him open the conversation. In addition, it was clear that I in Position 1 did not know how much the client knew about psychometrics already. So as a result, I made a phone call to check out his previous experience of testing, and when I got into the client meeting, it was calm, comfortable and en pointe.

So you can use this approach to programme your thinking to bring your impact to meet with your intention. This could be for:

- A business meeting as described above
- A difficult conversation
- An interview
- A presentation

The more you experience yourself doing something successfully, the more likely it is to happen. Remember the Positive Belief Cycle in Chapter 4 and Muhammed Ali's 'Future History'?

ENDNOTES

1. Breaking state: this simply means to get yourself out of that mindset to allow you to take up the next position cleanly.

2. Ecology check – looking at how the changes you are making impact on the other people/processes involved.

Exercise:

Take some time to try out the exercise detailed in this Chapter. Ideally, if you know someone with NLP training get them to take you through it first and they can facilitate the process, allowing you to get on with just experiencing it.

If you are already familiar with Perceptual Positions, then this might be the time to have a go with:

- Asking the question sequence
- Including the other people present
- Exploring different resourceful positions
- Applying the process to new situations

KEY POINTS:

» When we look at situations purely from our own viewpoint, it is unsurprisingly difficult to appreciate another person's perspective and therefore to make improvements

» To understand others better, approach them with more empathy, step 'into their shoes'. The change in you is likely to influence them positively

» Getting feedback from others about how they have experienced us is not always possible, particularly if the interaction has not happened yet

» Grinder and De Lozier developed an exercise called Perceptual Positions based on the therapists they modelled, which has become probably one of the most often used NLP exercises

» You can have someone else take you through this process or do it for yourself

» The exercise is best done kinaesthetically because of the strong link between learning and moving, and the spatial anchoring (i.e. the special association linked with a particular space)

» The process can be used to understand the impact of your behaviour and to put you 'at cause' to discover what would work better

» The process can be used for past or future interactions

Chapter 9
Helping Others...
Shut Up, Listen,
Appreciate!

"Setting an example is not the main means of influencing others, it is the only means."

Albert Einstein

HOW CAN MY IMPACT HELP OTHERS AROUND ME TO THRIVE?

Up to this point in the book, my focus has been on becoming more aware of our impact on others and getting into a resourceful state; and although both of these are aimed at improving other people's experience of us, and having our intention and impact matching more closely... the primary beneficiary is ourselves.

In this chapter, the aim is to be more outward looking and being more mindful of the leadership we can give to others whether in a work environment or elsewhere, as a manager or a colleague, as a friend or a neighbour. In Chapter 4 I referred to the pre-supposition:

We cannot not communicate

How we behave and what we say habitually around other people does not just influence their opinion of us, as Einstein points out it can also be a powerful example. Indeed more than that, what we choose to do and how we do it, can develop other people's thinking to help them to thrive and be at their best.

In Chapter 5 I looked at the effect of feedback: both how we give feedback effectively to others and how we can handle the feedback we receive. Specifically, I referred to the impact of feedback on the human brain and how it can "develop stronger neural networks that support inner strengths". Now I would like to look a little closer at some of the neuroscience and draw out what else we can do to help others thrive.

HOW DO THREAT AND REWARD AFFECT OUR BRAIN?

Earlier I referred to the fact that our reactions are tied up with our 'Stone Age' survival strategies which can cause 21st Century humans a few problems. Our brain is programmed for survival which means it needs to avoid threats and seek out rewards. The threat response needs to be stronger and faster, otherwise, we wouldn't be around to enjoy the rewards!

When we feel threatened, whether the threat is physical, emotional or verbal, our stress hormone cortisol increases and a chemical called dopamine is reduced. Blood flows away from the area of our brain where we do our thinking and planning and to the area that gets us ready for fight, flight or freeze. The result is we don't think so clearly, our decision making is impaired, our memory is reduced, we are distracted and we feel more anger. Another aspect of the threat response is that it is also longer lasting than our reward response. Just think about a time someone made a critical remark to you compared to when someone gave you a compliment... how long did you think about each?

Fairly obviously to create a threat response in someone else will not only be damaging to the relationship, it also impairs the effectiveness of that person and probably others around them.

On the other hand, when something good or pleasurable happens the neurotransmitter chemical dopamine is increased. Dopamine is responsible for transmitting signals between neurons in the brain, in effect increasing the number of new connections being made; so it is significant in our learning process. It also impacts on our perception, movement, memory and mood. Our brain likes dopamine and will look for ways to increase it. The effect on behaviour of this reward response is to make people more positive, focussed, willing to collaborate with others, able to think creatively and learn more easily.

In contrast to the threat, anything that we do to create the reward response in another person will not only enable them to be at their best, it will have significant impact on the task in hand and others around them too.

WHAT CAN I DO TO STIMULATE THE REWARD RESPONSE IN OTHERS?

In her book "Neuroscience for Organizational Change" Hilary Scarlett sets out ideas for keeping people performing at their best. I will explain how I apply these in the context of the training courses I run, although as you will see they are easily used in other settings too:

- *Focus on what is going well:* often at the start of courses, (particularly if participants are not universally delighted to be there), I ask each person to introduce themselves by sharing something that is going well for them at home or work. This question sometimes gets people laughing (another dopamine generator), in spite of initial reluctance in some cases, and gets them into a more positive state of mind for learning.

- *Appreciative feedback:* I have already referred to this else-where, and so important is it, that I am happy to repeat it. A standard element in most of my courses is to get each person paying attention to the contribution of others and giving that as feedback at the end of the day. Whilst delegates do not always find this an easy exercise to do at first, the effect of hearing verifiable complimentary feedback about themselves shows immediately in their confidence and involvement.

- *Recognising achievement:* when I am working with a group over a number of sessions each subsequent session starts with a review, where delegates can reflect on their learning so far and share how they have applied it in their work and their personal lives. This boosts their confidence and encourages them to take on the new learning in each successive module. For me, these are some of the most rewarding and moving times in my working life, (so my dopamine levels are soaring too).

- *Quick wins and short-term goals:* this relates to the point above. Delegates being able to achieve something quickly, and see that they are making progress, really gives them a good feeling. This is particularly important when a group are undertaking a longer programme of development; being able to mark their progress along the way gives a sense of achievement and keeps them on track for the bigger goal. In a small way, this is evident when I run courses on Time Management, where I encourage people to create 'Will Do' lists (i.e. a list that is realistically achievable in a typical working day), instead of 'To Do' lists that grow as the day progresses. There is a huge satisfaction in crossing off each item and seeing the list getting shorter, and even better completing it by the end of the working day.

- *Let them know what's happening:* our brains like information and to be able to predict what is likely to happen.

Uncertainty, on the other hand, can create a threat response. So the pre-course joining instructions set out what is covered and I go through the agenda at the start of each course I take, giving the opportunity for questions. A common question is to check if there is any role play planned – I explain there will be activities to practice, and they will be stretching, but role plays there will be none. A threat response severely damages a person's learning and engagement and the idea of role play in my experience has this exact effect.

- **Stimulation through novelty:** an essential ingredient when designing a course is to keep participants focussed, and this requires a variety of activities. While the brain does not like too much change or uncertainty, something is necessary to pique and maintain the group's interest. One of the ways I do this is to ask them at the beginning to set the 'Ground Rules' for the course – this hands control and responsibility for the learning to the group and brings in each person's participation early on. Other 'novelties' might include drawing, quizzes even body sculptures!

- **Laughter and chocolate (and/or fruit):** in Chapter 3, I pointed out the importance of the *Free Child* (the fun creative side of our personality), as being important to our well-being particularly in the work environment. The same is true on a training course and laughter has been demonstrated to increase productivity. The addition of chocolate or fruit to the mix has a similar effect. When new delegates remark on the copious amounts of chocolate on my courses, I reply "This job is too dangerous without chocolate!" (My attempt at humour). I must also take this opportunity to thank the delegates who bring cakes with them on courses... I hope they are reading this and realising their own brilliance in generating dopamine in others!

- **Creating opportunities to think:** while the brain craves information we do not want other people to do all our thinking for us. We don't like 'to be told' either. This probably reminds us of the *Parent* ego state also described in Chapter 3. As adults, we like to have information certainly and also have the opportunity to read, reflect and think for ourselves. So on courses, I sometimes suggest pre-course reading and create exercises where delegates can discuss and reach their own conclusions about how to apply the course material to their own work situation.

- **Creative spaces:** Nancy Kline, whose work I have long admired and will refer to later in this chapter, says that the place where people gather to think and work must say 'they matter'. This is something I bear in mind when choosing venues for my courses and something I place a lot of emphasis on when working with clients. I am fortunate to live close to The Lake District in Cumbria, where I run courses with the lakes and fells as a backdrop, and outdoor space to work in (weather permitting!). My room layout for a course is typically to banish the tables that can evoke 'school room' associations, to allow participants to move around more easily and converse as adults.

I am wondering if this has given you some ideas how you can create a reward response for others around you... or recognise why what you are already doing is working well?

HOW ELSE CAN MY BEHAVIOUR BRING OUT THE BEST IN OTHERS?

In Chapter 3, I described the *Adult* ego state and the positive effects behaving in this way can bring to a relationship. The *Adult* ego state is usually considered synonymous with assertive behaviour, but what does that mean exactly …and what do we need to be doing more of or differently in our dealings with others?

When we are behaving assertively, we are clear about our own wants and needs whilst being mindful of others' rights, wants and needs also. This can be a tricky balance to strike, and when I hear people talking about assertive behaviour, there is a strong emphasis on the assertive person being the one 'stating what I want'. Accordingly, there seems to be less recognition that to be truly assertive, this needs to be balanced with 'responsive' behaviours. Responsive behaviours are really paying attention to what the other person is saying (and the accompanying emotions) and asking questions to understand their viewpoint fully.

The balance can be tipped either way: too much of the assertive 'what I want/think' behaviour will come across aggressively and is likely to provoke a threat response in another person. As detailed earlier in this chapter, that can mean an aggressive defensive response which is all about winning and the person becomes hard, if not impossible to reason with. Alternatively, this can also result in the flight or freeze response where the other person goes quiet or gives in and keeps their ideas or opinions to themselves. Neither are particularly resourceful states in modern life where the 'threat' is perceived rather than real.

On the other hand, if the scales are tipped the other way, and there is too much responsive behaviour this can come across as passive, even submissive. As a result, the other person's thoughts and opinions are allowed to dominate; no challenge or new thinking is coming their way which can mean they learn nothing and even become bored or frustrated.

HOW CAN I CREATE AN ENVIRONMENT WHERE PEOPLE CAN THINK?

This idea of balance in communicating, to help ourselves and others to think is expanded beautifully in Nancy Kline's book "Time to Think". She talks about the 10 components of 'Creating a Thinking Environment' two of which I would like to draw attention to here. In Nancy's model, there is a balance between having equal opportunity to speak and holding different views from others, with really paying *Attention* to what someone else is saying and asking questions to both understand their viewpoint and develop their thinking. So let's look at Attention and Asking Questions more closely:

Attention: I have had the privilege of working with Nancy Kline on several occasions, and she says that:

> *"The quality of your attention determines the quality of other people's thinking."*

She also points out that the average time we have in conversation before someone else interrupts us with their questions or thoughts is about 15 seconds. As a result, our thinking is taken off in a different direction before we have fully expressed it. Paying attention is more than merely listening: it is about maintaining comfortable, interested eye contact with the person speaking, reacting appropriately without interrupting and holding your own thoughts in check until they have expressed theirs. Most people find this an unusual experience in a world where attention is often drawn by electronic devices, other distractions or even our thoughts. My experience is that it is not merely an act of self-control and generosity; it is one that allows other people to think for themselves and feel respected. It is common when I have paid attention in this way that the other person's thinking is expanded often coming up with solutions to their own issues without any suggestion from me.

On one occasion a course delegate said to me "I've been watching you – I ask you a question and you just look at me and don't say anything... I then start answering the question for myself... which means I knew the answer all along anyway!" We both just laughed.

Asking Questions: Nancy specifically refers to what she calls 'incisive questions', i.e. questions to respectfully challenge another's thinking which may be limiting them. She says:

"Our thinking, feeling, decision-making and action are driven by assumptions. The good ideas and feelings come from true liberating assumptions. The bad ones come from untrue limiting assumptions."

So asking questions is a way of truly understanding someone else's thinking, and it can also be about freeing them from 'limiting assumptions' that may be holding them back. This is very much in the same way that identifying the NLP 'Meta-Model' patterns set out in Chapter 6 can really help others to think differently. Too often the 'questioning' that people experience is another way of the questioner expressing their own view or their disagreement. When we ask questions in a responsive way, that is with respect, curiosity and giving them time to answer we invite people to think for themselves also.

You will also recognise when we pay attention to others and ask questions in this way, it not only impacts on their thinking, it is likely to strongly influence their behaviour towards us when we start to speak. In this way helping others to think and to thrive helps to do the same for us.

Exercise:

- Consider how you could apply the 'Reward Response' ideas in your own life and work or how you have been applying these already, knowingly or unknowingly

- Practice paying *Attention* to someone in a work or social context if they are presenting you with a problem or a dilemma that they have. Instead of coming in with your ideas or questions allow them to talk and use you as a sounding board. It may help to let them know at the outset that you will just listen without interruption as they talk it through.
  - Notice the self-control it may take to do this
  - Notice the effect on how they think about their issue

KEY POINTS:

» How we habitually choose to behave influences other people and their behaviour

» How we behave towards others can create a 'threat' or a 'reward' response in their brains

» The 'threat' response can come even if the threat is a perceived one and not an actual threat. It increases the stress hormone cortisol and directs blood away from the thinking part of the brain to the area responsible for 'flight and flight'. It is a state therefore where we react rather than think.

» The 'reward' response increases the neurotransmitter chemical dopamine, which the brain likes and will actively seek out ways to increase it. In this case, we tend to think better and more creatively, and are likely to be more collaborative with others.

» We can take specific actions to increase the 'reward' response in others which will keep them motivated and facilitate the learning process

» Behaving assertively is synonymous with the Adult ego state described in Chapter 3 and it is about achieving a balance between assertive and responsive behaviours

» Many people easily identify assertion as strongly putting your own view forward and less often recognise that this needs to be balanced by paying attention to the views of others and asking questions to understand

» Asking questions is also about respectfully challenging limiting assumptions which may be holding someone back

» When we pay attention and ask questions in this way we 'win a hearing for ourselves'

Chapter 10
It's In My Hands

---

*"What are the consequences of thinking
that your intelligence or personality is something you can develop, as opposed to something that is a fixed deep-seated trait?"*

Carol Dweck PhD, Professor of Psychology Stanford University

WHAT NOW... HOW MUCH OF MY IMPACT CAN I CHANGE?

I am wondering as I start this final chapter what led you to read this book? I am guessing that it was because you wanted to understand the point behind the title, or maybe that you already knew there was a gap between your intention and your impact and you wanted to know what you could do about it. Whatever your reason, I like to think that somewhere there is a belief that you can do something to make a change for yourself and others, which is a very powerful mindset to adopt.

Remember this formula of Jack Canfield's from Chapter 3:

$$E + R = O$$

Event/Experience + Our Reaction = Outcome

The key point is that what we choose to do or choose not to do is crucial. In each chapter, I have shared the learning and thinking and experiences that have been important in shaping my reactions and therefore my outcomes so far (there is much more learning out there I am looking forward to!). Hence my strong belief that what happens is 'in my hands'. It is not always that straightforward, however, and often I have been unaware at the time of the blocks I have put in my own way. In thinking that I couldn't do something I thought I was being realistic, not realising how this was limiting me.

> *"In order to be a realist, you must*
> *believe in miracles."*
>
> David Ben-Gurion, the first Prime Minister of Israel

At the start of this book, I used the metaphor of being inside a house and not knowing how it is viewed from the outside. And yet sometimes we are so familiar with the furnishings inside we don't always see when it is time to refurbish or update them until we look at them through someone else's eyes. A friend commented to me recently that she only noticed how scuffed her skirting boards were when she was showing someone else pictures of her children and saw the skirting boards in the background!

Our mindsets can be like this. Carol Dweck, the psychologist, quoted above, researches why people succeed and how to foster success. She has identified two mindsets: a 'fixed' mindset and a 'growth' mindset. In the first we limit ourselves by seeing our intelligence and capabilities as set in stone and in the second, we believe that these are things that we can grow and develop. Put simply she considers our ability to grow is determined by what we believe, and what we believe is also a choice. First of all, though, we have to actually recognise when we are doing something that might be holding us back before we can choose to change it.

HOW CAN I RECOGNISE 'FIXED' AND 'GROWTH' MINDSETS IN MYSELF?

Do you think that 'the kind of person' you are is set or do you think that you are always capable of change if you want to ? If you agree with the first part of the statement this suggests a 'fixed' mindset where you believe that this is how you are and you cannot do much about it. If you agreed with the second part of the statement, this suggests a 'growth' mindset i.e. one that believes that we have the potential to learn and grow.

When we have a 'fixed' mindset, Carol suggests we are always trying to prove ourselves and get worried about being wrong and making mistakes. When we have a 'growth' mindset, we see mistakes not as failing but as learning. This is the same idea as the 'Discovery Frame' in NLP, i.e. when we set a course or a meeting within a Discovery Frame, the objective is to create a safe space for learning where it is ok to make mistakes, rather than being the best or getting an exercise right first time. Often the people that make most mistakes get the most learning, as long as they feel they are in an environment where they are 'safe' to do so. In everyday life we can permit ourselves to accept that struggle and mistakes are part of the learning process too, and balancing this by recognising that we have responsibilities for our mistakes and to learn from them. We can extend this to others also and create a 'safe' space for them to grow.

It should be noted though that having a 'growth' mindset does not necessarily mean we could be the next Einstein or Mozart simply given the right attitude; it does mean though that our potential is unknown and unknowable and believing we can learn and grow is essential for tapping into it. In effect, we are creating our own 'Thinking Environment' and getting our Captain and Crew (conscious and unconscious minds) working together.

CAN I DEVELOP A GROWTH MINDSET?

"I don't divide the world into the weak and the strong, or the successes and the failures, those who make it or those who don't. I divide the world into learners and non-learners."

Benjamin R. Barber, political theorist and author

We can decide which 'camp' we want to be in once we realise where we may be limiting ourselves. It may be that we have a 'growth' mindset about some things in our life and a 'fixed' mindset on others. Making a shift from one to the other can have amazing results.

An example of this is playing the game of Scrabble. At one time I grumbled when I got 'bad letters', and my opponent seemed to have the all high scoring ones. This is a fixed mindset putting my lack of success down to my bad luck. What made the difference, (ok I admit, I still complain when I get too many vowels), was realising that it wasn't about who got the high scoring letters, but what I could do to take advantage of those letters once they have been played on the board: this is a growth mindset.

So we are capable of changing our thinking and changing our mindset, in the same way as we can adopt the pre-suppositions of NLP set out in Chapter 4. The concept of neuroplasticity[1] has been mentioned on several occasions throughout this book. This means that when we believe we can learn and grow, and put in the effort to do so, we are making changes to our brain. It is also believed that our ability to do this can last a lifetime.

So what indicators might we notice that indicate a 'fixed' mindset – here are some you may recognise:

- I won't apply for that job, I know I wouldn't get it anyway
- I am struggling with this task. I shouldn't have started it
- That presentation was embarrassing – I am not putting myself in that situation again
- I wasn't given a proper brief by my manager
- Leaders are born not made
- My teacher said I was a gifted child
- There is no point in joining a team that is not winning

A 'growth' mindset, on the other hand, is once again about putting yourself 'at Cause' rather than 'at Effect' asking questions like:

- What can I do to prepare myself for that role? Who can help me?
- What have I learnt so far? What will achieving this mean for me?
- What could I do differently next time? Who can give me some feedback?
- What questions do I need to ask? What would a 'proper brief' look like?
- How can I develop my leadership skills? What have I achieved already?

- I wonder in what other ways I could be gifted that I haven't tried yet?
- What could I bring to the team to be part of turning things around?

And it is not just about us – asking these kinds of questions respectfully of other people will help encourage a 'growth' mindset in others too.

"They always say time changes things, but you actually have to change them yourself."
Andy Warhol

In fact, each chapter of this book has been about encouraging a growth mindset in ourselves, and deliberately or otherwise, in others too. As I sat down to finish this book today, I got this message from my long time friend Alyson Renwick, a Nurture Teacher in Glasgow, who has been reviewing the book for me. I think it is a beautiful example of how applying just one thing, and thereby changing our own thinking and behaviour, makes a huge impact for ourselves and those around us:

"I loved the Attention piece...I'm constantly applying your advice to my work situations where colleagues frequently come to me, and I try so hard to listen carefully... you'll know how hard that is for me!! But the results are as you said... they frequently self–solve... if someone listens to me properly... the same thing happens to me... this might be my favourite chapter!!"

TO A 'GROWTH' MINDSET AND BEYOND!

Every chapter of this book is intended to focus practically on what we can do to bring our impact to meet with our good intentions: in doing so, we can make a real difference for ourselves and others. While I work with NLP and train NLP courses, I have included other work and ideas that have given me insight and inspiration, as I see how all of these sit together and complement one another.

In fact, this whole book has been an object lesson in developing a 'growth mindset' for me too. The idea was first suggested to me some years ago by a delegate on a course and has been repeated to me by others since... all met with the internal response *"I can't do that."* (I hope my external response was more polite.) It eventually dawned on me that their suggestions were in fact feedback, and they saw or anticipated something that I did not see in myself... and so at that point my thinking switched to *"What if I could do that... there might be something I have to say, that others might want to read and find useful".* Abandoning the fixed mindset thinking of 'this has to be perfect' I started, and each Chapter has been a learning process for me too along the way. Adopting a growth mindset has also shown me something else: the response of other people, who have encouraged me and taken time to review each chapter and make suggestions and comments. And so now my thinking is *"What else can I do... and how can I start?"* which is an approach that I can apply in so many other areas of my life, where a 'fixed' mindset might be lurking. So I hope you have enjoyed my first book, and that there has been something in these Chapters to inspire your 'growth' mindset too... thank you for reading!

"Walk on air against your better judgement."

Inscribed on Seamus Heaney's headstone from

his poem "The Gravel Walks."

ENDNOTES

1. Neuroplasticity: the capacity of the brain to develop and change throughout life, something Western science once thought impossible —Time, 8 May 2006

Exercise:

- From reading the descriptions of the 'mindsets' which do you identify with most strongly ?

- Whatever the result from this… consider where you may have a 'fixed' mindset in your life or work. Do you want to change it and if so what is your first step/question to move yourself from a 'fixed' to a 'growth' mindset

KEY POINTS:

» What you choose to do or choose not to do will determine the outcome in a situation

» Thinking you are being realistic that you cannot do something may actually be you limiting yourself

» We may be unaware of how we are holding ourselves back

» Carol Dweck has developed the idea that we have 'fixed' and 'growth' mindsets

» A 'Fixed' mindset sees our intelligence and capabilities as set in stone and therefore limited

» A 'Growth' mindset sees that our potential is unknown and unknowable but that we can tap into our potential by believing we can learn and grow

» When we recognise we have a 'fixed' mindset about something we can change it and develop a 'growth' mindset instead, and we can help others do the same

Exercise – Applying Your Learning From This Book:

- Take some time to notice what you have used so far from this book… it may be that you have shifted your thinking in some way, or like my friend Alyson applied a different way of behaving. What difference has this made for you and others so far?

- Consider then what you would like to apply now, and where you can start
  - What change do you envisage this will create?
  - See the outcome(s) you are aiming for, what you will be hearing and feeling when you have achieved them?

Finally, I would love it if you would like to share with me how you have used this book… I am in a 'growth' mindset too! You can email me at info@florencemadden.co.uk

Sources and Further Reading

LUFT, J. **Of Human Interaction: Johari Model** Mayfield Publishing Company (1969)

JAMES, T. AND WOODSMALL, W. **Time line Therapy and the Basis of Personality** Meta Publications U.S. First edition (1988)

HARRIS, T.A. MD **I'm OK-You're OK** Pan Books (1973)

STEWART, I. AND JOINES, V. **TA Today** Lifespace Publishing (1987)

CANFIELD, J. **The Success Principles: How to Get From Where You Are to Where You Want to Be** William Morrow & Company; 10th Anniversary ed. edition (2015)

DILTS, R.B. **Visionary Leadership Skills** Meta Publications Inc (1996)

BURGESS, F. **The Bumper Book of Modelling** Kilmonivaig Publishing (2014)

MALTZ, M. MD FICS **Psycho-Cybernetics** Perigee Books; Updated and Expanded edition (2015)

HANSON, R. PhD **Just One Thing: Developing a Buddha Brain One Simple Practice at a Time** New Harbinger Publications; Original edition (October 1, 2011)

ROSENTHAL, R. and JACOBSON, L. **Pygmalion In The Classroom** Holt, Reinhart and Winston (1968)

KLINE, N. **Time To Think** Cassell Publishing (2002)

NELSON, N.C. PhD **The Power of Appreciation In Business** Mindlab Publishing (2005)

GOLEMAN, D. **Social Intelligence: The New Science of Human Relationships** Arrow Publishing (2007)

GALLWEY, W.T. **The Inner Game of Tennis** Pan Books, Revised (2015)

CAULFIELD, M. **The Meta Model Demystified** CreateSpace Independent Publishing Platform; 2nd edition (2014)

GAWAIN, S. **Creative Visualization** New World Library; New edition (2002)

JAMES, T. MS PhD and SHEPHARD, D BSc DES **Presenting Magically** Crown House Publishing (2001)

JAMES, M.B. MA PhD **Integrate The Shadow, Master Your Path** Balboa Press (2014)

BARGH, J. PhD **Before You Know It: The Unconscious Reasons We Do What We Do** William Heinemann (2017)

HANNAFORD, C. PhD **Smart Moves: Why Learning Is Not All In Your Head** Great Ocean Publishers (1995)

ROBBINS, A. **Unlimited Power: The New Science of Personal Achievement** Simon & Schuster UK; New edition (2001)

SHERVINGTON, M. **Don't Think of Purple Spotted Oranges!** Marshall Editions (2000)

SCARLETT, H. **Neuroscience For Organisational Change** Kogan Page (2016)

DWECK, C.S. **Mindset: How You Can Fulfil Your Potential** Robinson (2012)

Baumeister, R., Bratslavsky, E., Finkenauer, C. & Vohs, K.D. **Bad Is Stronger Than Good** Review of General Psychology 2001. Vol. 5. No. 4. 323-370

About Florence Madden

Hello, I am Florence Madden a trainer and coach and a native of Northern Ireland who has made Cumbria home. With such a lovely location, I am fortunate to spend a substantial part of my working life running open courses in the Lake District since starting my business Florence Madden Associates back in 2002. I also develop and deliver bespoke courses for clients who are based all over the UK.

I am fortunate too to do work I love, and I am thrilled to see what people can do and achieve when they believe in themselves and treat others with respect. The maxim from Johann Wolfgang Goethe that

I quote in this book is one that has been demonstrated over and over by the people I have worked with through the years:

"If I accept you as you are I will make you worse, however if I treat you as though you are what you are capable of becoming, I will help you become that."

I have also been blessed in my working life and in my development, to have others who believed in what I was capable of becoming too – even or maybe especially, when I could not see it for myself. This book is an example of just that: a number of clients over the years have suggested I 'write this stuff down' and eventually I listened to them. (There is a big piece of learning for me in this too i.e. to listen sooner!).

I have learnt and been inspired by quite a number of people and ideas and this eclectic range of influences is apparent as you read through the book. I am an NLP Trainer and am delighted how NLP blends and connects with other concepts. Apart from when I am running NLP certificated courses, my bespoke courses are a blend of what works in my experience.

You can find out more about the services I offer and the courses I run on my website:

www.florencemadden.co.uk

And also… about my second book "Everyday NLP" which has been co-written with my friend, associate and inspiration Eleni Sarantinou, who has encouraged me to be the best version of myself since we first met.

I wonder who you too will help and inspire as you implement the ideas in this book? I would love to hear your story… contact me on:

info@florencemadden.co.uk

So many people to thank...

I do not know where to start so I will just start!

Thank you to some of the inspirational trainers that I have had the privilege of working with Sarah Frossell, Sue Knight, Nancy Kline, Robert Dilts, Stephen Gilligan and John Grinder.

Thank you to Louise Fisher who first introduced me to NLP years ago and showed me what quality feedback can do. Also to Maggie Crighton whose energy and belief in me has been ever-present since I allegedly sat on her sofa and said "Giza job" over 25 years ago.

Thank you to the friends, and the clients who have become friends, and now editors, who have given their time generously to bring this book to publication. Especially thanks to them for respecting me enough to give the corrections as well as the praise... I needed both: Claire Bradshaw, Chris Bray, Laura Cadman, Maureen Tallis,

Dr Jo Verrill, Nicky Ellis, Alyson Renwick, Eleni Sarantinou and Dr David Fraser.

Thank you to my lovely Mum and Dad whose encouragement shaped my life and they would be thrilled that I finally wrote a book!

And finally to my lovely husband Pat who has celebrated every learning and success with me down the years… and who frequently reminds me of what I still need to learn about making my impact reflect my intention!!

Lightning Source UK Ltd.
Milton Keynes UK
UKHW02f0700251018
331176UK00011B/1448/P